T0336429

ADVANCE PRAISE FOR
The Auschwitz Protocols: Ceslav Mordowicz
and the Race to Save Hungary's Jews

"A compelling account of life at Auschwitz, combined with a suspenseful story of a rare escape from that monstrous monument to evil, *The Auschwitz Protocols* offers precious insight into the unspeakable tragedy that was the Holocaust."

—**David I. Kertzer**, Paul Dupee, Jr. University Professor of Social Science, Professor of Italian Studies at Brown University, and 2015 Pulitzer Prize-winning author of *The Pope and Mussolini: The Secret History of Pius XI and the Rise of Fascism in Europe*

"Fred Bleakley sought to chronicle what had been entrusted to him a couple decades ago by Ceslav Mordowicz, an escapee from the Auschwitz death camp. The author has fulfilled his witness mission: to present to us the truth about this story that has caused much controversy to this day. A very skilled and accomplished journalist, he sheds light on interesting hitherto unknown details and contexts, while basing his views on important document sources. We owe him thanks for his determination, perseverance, and commitment. His book is an outstandingly interesting read."

—**Zoltán Tibori-Szabó**, Habilitated Doctor, Professor at the Babes-Bolyai University of Cluj, Romania, and Director of the Institute for Holocaust and Genocide Studies of the same university

"*The Auschwitz Protocols* follows the life of Ceslav Mordowicz who, together with Aronst Rosin, escaped from Auschwitz in May, 1944, and brought details of the Hungarian deportations to the outside world. The incredible escape of the two prisoners from Auschwitz is vividly described. This is an invaluable book, especially to a generation of young people who don't recognize the word 'Auschwitz.'"

—**John H. Merey**, survivor from wartime Budapest who, with his Jewish family, was on the Kasztner Train that transported them and other Jews to safety in June, 1944. He is now a medical doctor in Florida.

"*The Auschwitz Protocols* is an excellent book. I wonder how many years it took to write on this difficult subject in such an accurate way. It is a very richly documented and extremely well-written page turner."

—**Avi Pazner**, son of Dr. Chaim Pozner, a Jewish leader in Switzerland who helped put pressure on Regent Horthy to stop deportations from Budapest. He currently lives in Israel and was Israeli Ambassador to France and Italy.

THE AUSCHWITZ PROTOCOLS

CESLAV MORDOWICZ
AND THE RACE TO SAVE
HUNGARY'S JEWS

FRED R. BLEAKLEY

A WICKED SON BOOK
An Imprint of Post Hill Press

The Auschwitz Protocols:
Ceslav Mordowicz and the Race to Save Hungary's Jews
© 2022 by Fred R. Bleakley
All Rights Reserved

ISBN: 978-1-63758-262-6
ISBN (eBook): 978-1-63758-263-3

Cover design by Tiffani Shea
Interior design and composition by Greg Johnson, Textbook Perfect

Post Hill Press
New York • Nashville
posthillpress.com

Published in the United States of America
1 2 3 4 5 6 7 8 9 10

To Jane and our son Will.
The best that ever happened to me.

CONTENTS

INTRODUCTION

On June 6, 1944, while the Allies were storming Normandy, thousands of Jewish men, women, and children from Hungary stumbled from cramped cattle car trains arriving at Auschwitz-Birkenau concentration camp. At the same time, two escapees from Auschwitz, Czeslaw (Ceslav)[1] Mordowicz, a twenty-four-year-old Polish Jew, and Arnost Rosin, a twenty-nine-year-old Slovakian Jew, were telling the local branch of the Bratislava Jewish Central Council (JCC) about the concentration camp. Beginning on May 15, they had seen, firsthand, the camp's daily arrival of up to 12,000 Hungarian Jews. The arriving deportees had endured days of stifling heat, a lack of water, and, in each car, one overflowing bucket of human waste. They lined up as they got off the trains, with German shepherd dogs howling at them, where a uniformed SS physician flipped his thumb right or left. The lucky few moved to the right, fit for labor. The others would soon be lying dead inside the camp's gas chambers. As one historian put it, the Hungarian Holocaust was "the most concentrated and methodical deportation and massacre program of the war, a slaughter machine that functioned, perfectly oiled, for forty-six days on end."[2]

The mass deportations of Hungary's remaining Jews ended on July 6 on the order of Hungary's leader Miklós Horthy. Just hours later they would have been rounded up from the center of Budapest for deportation to Auschwitz.[3] Ceslav Mordowicz played a catalytic role in making that happen. This is Mordowicz's story: from the start of the war, his life in the ghetto, and his year and a half in Auschwitz, to his harrowing escape and cunning ways of avoiding recapture until he was finally caught, only to be deported in a nightmarish return to Auschwitz. This is also the story of Mordowicz's determination to tell of the horrors of Auschwitz. By doing so, his and his partner's testimony corroborated the gruesome reports of two prior Auschwitz successful escapes, that of Walter Rosenberg (Rudolf Vrba) and Alfred "Fredo" Wetzler on April 7, 1944, and that of Jerzy Tabeau, known as the "Polish Major," six months earlier. Those previous escapees had not been taken seriously until then by the officials who could make a difference.[4] Together, the accounts of those three escapees have become the now famous Auschwitz Protocols, released by the US War Refugee Board to widespread press coverage in late 1944 and used by the prosecution in the postwar Nuremberg war trials of Nazi leaders.

In the decades following the war, historians and documentary filmmakers have focused largely on the Vrba/Wetzler report for the international pressure on Horthy to protect Hungary's remaining Jews. The importance of the Vrba/Wetzler report, as well as that of the "Polish Major" Tabeau, is irrefutable. However, the significance of the Mordowicz/Rosin Auschwitz report in corroborating and drawing further attention to those two reports has not been sufficiently recognized. A major reason stems from misstatements in the introduction of the Auschwitz Protocols. The misstatements by the War Refugee Board (WRB) are detailed in the coda of this book. In contrast, my research shows that the Mordowicz/Rosin report gave religious and Allied officials more reason to see the truth of Auschwitz and put pressure on Horthy to save his country's remaining Jews.

I first heard of Ceslav in 1995, after Union College history professor Stephen Berk gave a lecture at a synagogue in Toronto. He cited Ceslav as an "unsung hero" of the war, adding that it wasn't known whether he was still alive. Hearing this, a woman in the audience rose and pointed to the man sitting beside her, saying, "Ceslav is right here!" A few months later, he received an honorary degree at Union College's graduation ceremony. As a writer at the *Wall Street Journal*, I attended the ceremony on a Sunday in June of that year to hear Union's president, Roger H. Hull, announce that Mordowicz "was one of four brave Jews. The news you and your fellow escapees brought helped alert the world to the horrors of the Nazi death camps." My short article on Mordowicz, published in the *Journal* the following week, led to the US Holocaust Museum interviewing Mordowicz for its archive of oral histories.[5] That article also put me on the road to writing this book. The sheer drama of the race to save the last Jews of Hungary captured my interest. Ceslav's story could not be told without the background of Hungary's on-again, off-again embrace of its Jewish population. I knew I needed to give the story "sweep and scope," as one of my former editors, John Lee of the *New York Times*, once stressed. But my day job and family came first. So I stored away all my interviews with Ceslav from 1995 to 1997 and waited until retirement several years ago to pursue the broader context of Ceslav's story.[6]

There have been several versions of this dramatic period written by Holocaust historians, most of them compiled decades after the war and delivered in an academic style. Many of these accounts differ on or leave vague the steps that led to

Horthy's decision. The questions about the timing of Horthy's knowledge of the Holocaust and the Hungarian administration's role in the deportations remain a hot debate, fueled by the current regime and its supporters to minimize Hungarian responsibility. My challenge was to read the literature, sift through the inconsistencies, delve into archives, and conduct interviews to render a reasonable account of the Hungarian Holocaust and the role Ceslav Mordowicz had in helping to save the Jews of Budapest.

Would the Vrba/Wetzler report have garnered the attention it deserved without the corroboration of Ceslav and Arnost's report? Was Ceslav Mordowicz, the leader of his escape with Rosin, just a bit player in Horthy's momentous decision? Had Professor Berk overreached when he referred to Mordowicz as an unsung hero? I did not come away with conclusive, cause-and-effect evidence that the Mordowicz/Rosin report prompted the appeals to Horthy by religious and political leaders. But it was obvious that the connection and chronology of the events preceded the order to end deportations.

I took some liberties in telling this story as a narrative nonfiction, rather than as a strictly historical account. But I did not alter, nor purposely omit, important facts. I also had a point to make in writing this book. A catalyst, which I believe Ceslav was in this case, can be the missing link essential to the outcome of a significant event. But catalysts are often overshadowed. I didn't want Ceslav to be forgotten or remembered only as a footnote in this remarkable chapter of history.

CHAPTER ONE

WAR COMES TO MŁAWA

Usually, when twenty-year-old Ceslav Mordowicz would sit down to the evening meal with his family at their modest home in Mława, a small city in northern Poland, the table talk was about the oddities of his father Herman's grain business or the always dramatic life of his sixteen-year-old sister, Rachel. Ceslav, who had graduated the Hebrew gymnasium at the top of his class, would sometimes add how close he was to earning enough money from tutoring high school students—he taught them math, science, and even German—to attend the University of Warsaw.

But the Thursday evening of August 31, 1939, was different. Anna, Ceslav's mother, put aside the apron she wore while dishing out leftover meat pierogis from the early afternoon main meal and brought up the topic of the day. The radio and newspapers had been speculating about a potential invasion of Poland by Germany, stemming from the pact that Germany and the Soviet Union had signed about a week earlier. Rumor had it that the two had agreed to partition Poland. Herman and Ceslav dove right into the discussion, but it frightened Rachel. So, the subject was dropped.

"I'm going out," Ceslav said after downing a glass of steeped black tea. There weren't any new Gary Cooper cowboy movies at the Mława cinema, so Ceslav planned on strolling around the town square with his friends. On several days of the week, Mława served as the hub of the region's agricultural trade. The square would bustle with farmers from nearby villages, whose horse-drawn wagons were filled with chickens, geese, turkeys, vegetables, and fruit. Peasants on foot carried straw baskets filled with butter and cheese, along with pies and pastries, to sell in the center of the open square.

The evenings were more relaxed. On his way to the square Ceslav passed a large rose garden in full bloom, a reminder, he thought, of all that is good. At about eight p.m., Ceslav found his friends in the square, which was lined with coffee houses, restaurants, a movie theater, and a tavern. It soon seemed like half of Mława was in the square, enjoying one of the last days of summer. Jews made up about a third of the city's population, but anti-Semitism had been growing since Poland's independence after WWI. Some non-Jews were urging neighbors not to frequent Jewish shops and fights between Jew and Christian youth groups were common in Mława's parks. Mława had had a Jewish community since the mid-sixteenth century and had come to be known for its Jewish intellectuals and philosophers. It was the birthplace of some of Poland's best writers and socialist politicians. Since the late nineteenth century it had also bred proponents of the Zionist movement, with their calls for a separate Jewish state. Ceslav and his family were of the modern sect of Orthodox Jews who would blend into society in manners and dress, rather than ultra-Orthodox, which is more conservative and reclusive.

The talk among Ceslav and his group of friends that evening kept returning to what Germany would do next. Germany had occupied the Czech lands, Bohemia and Moravia, in March 1939, shredding the Munich Pact that it had signed with Britain, France, and Italy in September 1938. This aggressive act prompted Britain and France's offer to guarantee the borders of Poland and Romania, which would mean war if Germany went any further. The nonaggression agreement signed by Germany and the Soviet Union on August 23, 1939, left little doubt that an attack on Poland was imminent. Some of Ceslav's friends held out hope, making bets with each other about whether England and France would ever let that happen. Little did they know that at that very moment, a million and a half German troops and 2,000 bombers and fighter planes were massed on the Polish border.

Ceslav still had to prepare for the next day's tutoring, so he said goodbye to his pals around 10:30, taking a longer route home to think about the conversations they'd had about Germany. It angered him that Adolf Hitler and the Nazis viewed Poles, and Jews especially, as racially inferior to Germans. He had learned their language in the summers as a youth vacationing with his family in Danzig (now Gdansk), a trading port on the Baltic Sea, where German was the regional language. And his friends sometimes kidded him that he might be German, since he looked like one. When Ceslav turned the corner and saw the lights on in his home at #8 Wojtowstwo Street, his thoughts turned to what would happen to his father, mother, and sister if Germany invaded Poland. Hours later, the sound of bombs exploding on the outskirts of Mława shook Ceslav from sleep. World War II had begun. Mława was in north central Poland, about ten miles southwest of the border of Prussia, the largest federal state in the German republic. By five in the morning, as the explosions grew louder, Ceslav could see fires rising from parts of Mława and scurried activity on the street below his second floor window.

Around dawn, low-flying German planes began strafing the city. Panic in homes and on the streets quickly turned into mass evacuation. Ceslav was amazed to see so many people so well organized, as if they all knew what to do and where to go. There were hardly any cars, just horse-drawn wagons and people on foot, many carrying babies while pushing their strollers stuffed with clothes, silverware, and their family's jewels. The Mordowicz family was hurriedly packing when Herman received a telephone call around seven in the morning from the foreman of Michael Steiner, a local farmer he knew well. The foreman told Herman that Steiner, a German, had been jailed several days earlier by the Polish military. Now, he, the foreman, and the five other farm workers did not know what to do or where to go. Herman, who had bought all the farm's grain for years, was the only friendly authority figure they knew. "Come fast to me," he said, telling the foreman to harness his largest wagon with strong horses. An hour later, the Mordowicz family climbed aboard the same wagon, which was already crowded with six farm workers. Heading out of Mława, they joined the throngs of families surging out of the city. German planes swooped down on them like easy prey. As shells blasted to the rear and sides of the wagon, the horses bucked. Ceslav wrapped his arm around his frightened sister.

"Turn into the field," yelled Herman, pointing the way to the foreman who controlled the reins. Herman knew where he was going. Steiner's brother, another one of Herman's grain suppliers, had a farm about twenty miles south of Mława. It took all day to get there. The road they left had become impassable from the bombs that were still falling behind and ahead of them. Finally, after cutting across one wheat or rye field after another, they spotted his farmhouse. Though he wanted to help, Michael Steiner's brother feared drawing too much attention from the Polish military because of what happened to his brother. He fed the group dinner and said, "Please, sleep in the garden shed tonight and take to the woods in the morning." The Mordowicz family and farm workers made space for themselves in the shed and bedded down. Herman hoped he could persuade the foreman to return to Mława the next day to see if their home had survived the shelling.

The following morning, Ceslav woke up and, stepping outside, saw German fighter planes flying through clouds of smoke rising from burning villages outside of Mława. Returning home was out of the question. "The war is following us," Ceslav told his family. The shed's inhabitants quickly gathered their belongings and ran into the nearby woods, where they hid the rest of the day and night under the cover of ash, maple, alder, and linden trees. Occasionally, Ceslav and his family would furtively dash into the fields to grab some carrots or potatoes, only to be sent fleeing back to the woods by machine-gunning planes.

Ceslav's father and the foreman walked out of earshot from their gypsy-like encampment that evening to discuss their next move. Herman said if his relatives in Warsaw were safe, they might help. The foreman was skeptical but agreed on the chance that he and his fellow workers could find jobs there. They set out again in the crowded wagon, stopping at farms along the seventy-five-mile journey to pick vegetables, all the while getting more and more depressed by the devastation they saw in one village after another. It took a week to get to Warsaw, interrupted by flights into the woods as Luftwaffe planes circled overhead. The weary group arrived in Warsaw just as night had fallen. Having left the workers with the horse and wagon on the outskirts of the city, Ceslav and his family trudged through block after block of the ruined city.

Seeing the raging fires and hearing the exploding bombs and human misery, Ceslav said to himself, "This is for Dante, not for me." The Germans were dropping more than 600 tons of bombs on Warsaw—at the time, the largest air raid in history. The combination of aerial bombardment and artillery fire reduced much of the historic city center to rubble. Buildings were falling like so many houses of cards. Ceslav and his family spent the night in the sheltered area of a courtyard. The next morning, Ceslav said he would go out to look for some food. He opened the gate to the courtyard and saw across the street a large building collapsed on all sides, still burning. Among the rubble he could see arms, legs, and three or four people half buried.

They were screaming. All of a sudden the last wall collapsed inwards—Mercifully, Ceslav thought—silencing their cries.

For the next three weeks, bombs fell incessantly on Warsaw. The Mordowicz family spent their days searching for places to hide, sleeping inside churches and the lobbies of still-standing apartment buildings. Food was scarce, and the vegetables they had gathered from farms on the trek to Warsaw soon ran out. Nothing worked: no telephones, no water, no power. It was a city under siege. "It's time to leave," Ceslav's father announced one morning. With Warsaw in ruins, he had abandoned hope of finding friends and relatives in the city. They needed to flee. But to where? The farm workers and their wagon had long gone. And so the hungry and despondent family had to walk to the only home they knew: Mława.

CHAPTER TWO

FATE STEPS IN

Without a wagon, the walk back to Mława was painfully slow for the weakened Mordowicz family. They shuffled mile after mile. While scavenging a farm for potatoes and carrots to eat on the fourth day of their trek, Ceslav and his sister Rachel wondered aloud to each other how they were going to survive. At least fifty miles still lay ahead. Suddenly, they both stopped what they were doing and looked at each other. Rachel spoke first, saying only the name "Shulamith." Ceslav knew exactly who Rachel meant: they could seek help from the family of one of her friends, Shulamith Perelmutter, who lived in Płońsk, a small city about thirty-seven miles south of Mława. He was already smitten with Shulamith, an eighteen-year-old blonde of medium height with blue eyes and a carefree manner. Rachel had introduced them a month earlier, and after a few days had gone by, Ceslav rode his bike from Mława to Płońsk for a visit. On his return ride, he was whistling and full of hope.

"Of course, how can I help?" Shulamith said when they showed up a few days later at the grocery store run by her divorced mother. They lived above the store with Shulamith's fifteen-year-old sister, Hadassa. Ceslav's heart beat a little faster as he took in Shulamith's warm and understanding smile. But he couldn't return it. More than a month on the run, hungry, sleeping in the woods or in shells of bombed-out homes had taken its toll. The thought that he and his family were filthy, probably smelled, and had the haggard look of starving beggars made him lower his head in embarrassment. "First, we need petroleum jelly to get rid of lice," Ceslav said shyly. "Then, please, a corner to get cleaned," he added, averting her eyes. Over the next two days, Ceslav was impressed with Shulamith's optimism and how she made him laugh by poking fun at his sorry state. As he regained his strength, he helped her stock the shelves in the store and watched as she slipped extra food into the bags of shoppers who could barely afford what little they had bought. Young and in love, Ceslav told his father, mother, and sister he would not be joining them on the journey to Mława. As they trudged off the next day, laden with baskets of food from Shulamith's mother, Ceslav waved goodbye with Shulamith at his side.

Ceslav became the much-needed male presence in Shulamith's family. To Hadassa, he was the big brother she always wanted, quick to take her side when she felt put upon by her older sister or mother. To Shulamith's mother, he was the smart, hard-working partner who kept the books, made deliveries, and relieved her of the burden of running a business alone. And to Shulamith, he was like the boy next door who grew up to be a handsome confidant who just might share her future. Not to mention, it was good to have a man in the house as German soldiers roamed the streets. In the weeks and months following the invasion, 1.5 million German soldiers took over the country. The Polish army folded quickly, including at the Battle of Mława, north of the city. Local resistance groups formed, but they, too, were no match for the Germans. When a half million Soviet soldiers arrived from the east that fall, the two invading forces carved up the country as originally planned.

Ordinary shopkeepers like Mrs. Perelmutter were left to ply their business, while German troops began rounding up professionals, politicians, professors, priests, journalists, land-owners—anyone in authority who might stir up protests or resistance. The deaths began right away. In September, there were 200 executions every day in Płońsk. "We could be next," Ceslav said to Shulamith as they heard the gunfire from a mass execution in the town square. But where could they go? The same thing was happening in villages and cities across Poland. Trapped, Ceslav and Mrs. Perelmutter went about their business. He was torn between joining the resistance and staying with Shulamith. Hoping that they might somehow escape Poland, he and Shulamith decided to get married. Europe's immigration laws at the time were difficult to navigate. As a married couple, they would stand a better chance of being accepted in a friendly country if they found a way out. In late 1940, a rabbi performed the ceremony in Ceslav's parents' home in Mława, surrounded by friends and relatives. Sadness and fear lingered behind the shouts of "mazel tov!" the traditional wish on such occasions for long health and happiness.

A few months later, shop after shop in Płońsk had to be turned over to German citizens. Hitler had written in his 1925 *Mein Kampf* manifesto that the destiny of Germany was to expand into Eastern Europe to provide living space for the German people. Mrs. Perelmutter's grocery store was taken over by Daniel Doring, a carpenter from Germany. In his late thirties, he arrived with instructions from his homeland to turn the store and its warehouse into a furniture factory. At first, Doring allowed Ceslav and the three females to continue living next to the factory in two small rooms. Doring didn't feel sympathy for the family; rather, he was impressed with Ceslav's industriousness. Doring had seen right away that Ceslav had the account books in perfect shape, was clearly advising Mrs. Perelmutter on the right amount of inventory to carry, and had a pleasant, but authoritative manner in handling difficult situations with suppliers and customers. He believed that the young man could help run the new factory, which would produce handmade furniture for delivery to Nazi officials locally and in Germany. Ceslav soon began taking care of the factory's books as the evolution of the grocery store to furniture factory took place.

"You don't look like a Jew," Doring told Ceslav one day. This was true. Handsome and blue-eyed and swept-back, light brown hair, Ceslav could have passed for an Aryan—especially since he spoke German fluently. That appearance would come in handy when life in Płońsk changed dramatically one day in May 1941. Ceslav heard commotion in the streets and saw German troops with drawn guns ordering the neighboring Jews from their homes. He, Mrs. Perelmutter, and her two daughters were the next family taken on a march to the poorest section of Płońsk. It was several square blocks of one-story buildings or abandoned warehouses where they would live with poor families who had no indoor plumbing. A seven-foot-high picket fence with barbed wire surrounded the ghetto, with guarded gates at the center of each side. Every day Ceslav saw the area become more crowded, with eventually 8,000 Jews and less and less food available at the central soup kitchen.

In Mława, Herman Mordowicz, Anna, and Rachel joined 6,500 Jewish neighbors in a similar ghetto around the same time. What surprised and disappointed Ceslav and both of his families was not that the Nazis took such harsh measures; it was the complicity of so many Christian neighbors who, to date, had not joined in the rising tide of anti-Semitism in Poland. Now, virtually no one objected to the ghetto segregations, and many non-Jewish Poles were quick to point out the hiding places of Jews the Nazis could not find.

Shulamith, as ever, saw a bright side to her new quarters, where she, Ceslav, her mother, and sister lived in one small room, six feet by twelve feet. They were fortunate. Some rooms only slightly larger housed two families. Although privacy was scarce, Ceslav and Shulamith made the most of the time her mother and Hadassa were out. After a while, they simply waited for intimacy until the two were asleep. No doubt, Hadassa was only pretending to sleep some of the time. Ceslav and other Jewish laborers had permits that allowed them to leave the ghetto in the morning for work and return in the late afternoon. Doring's business was growing so rapidly he needed a manager for his factory.

Ceslav—the smartest, best organized, and most well-liked of Doring's forty employees—was the obvious choice. But given that the factory's manager would deal directly with high-profile customers, such as the town's mayor and the local Reich commandant, he could not be a known Jew. Doring hit upon a ruse. Ceslav would be called a *volksdeutscher*, meaning he was Polish but of German, non-Jewish descent. Each morning as he left the ghetto, Ceslav would unpin the Jewish stars from the front and back of his clothing, hide them in his pockets, and put them back on before walking through the ghetto's gates each evening. "I am a double agent," he told Shulamith. "By day, I am a German Christian, but by night I am a Polish Jew." Shulamith laughed. "Don't get your days and nights mixed up," she joked.

In addition to overseeing all the factory workers, Ceslav, along with Doring, was the public face of the business. "Heil Hitler!" the Reich commandant would shout each day to Ceslav from outside his office down the street from the furniture factory. Doring had told the commandant that Ceslav was German. As far as the commandant was concerned, that made him one of the favored few in Płońsk. Ceslav's stomach churned with anxiety every time he saw the stiff arm rise, but somehow he managed never to return it. Ceslav wondered why he was allowed to pass without suspicion. Perhaps it was the Germanic airs he assumed, such as the brown leather jacket he wore or the feather he kept in his Tyrolean cap. Ceslav flourished in his job at the factory while fewer and fewer of his fellow Jews were allowed to earn a living. By the end of 1941, after six months trapped in the ghetto, many families had run out of money to pay the SS for food. Ceslav devised a plan to help them. Thanks to the local commandant, who would regularly bribe Ceslav to expedite the delivery of furniture to his fellow officers back home, Ceslav had access to scarce luxuries like bacon and cigarettes. He also had plenty of cash, as he had convinced Doring to increase the salaries of all his employees, including Ceslav. He used his money to buy food from Christian storekeepers and stockpiled it along with the gifts he received from the commandant. How could he smuggle the supplies into the ghetto? The furniture factory produced just what he needed: cabinets.

Ceslav filled newly made cabinets with food and arranged to have them emptied near a secret entrance to the ghetto. It was around a corner from the main entrance where there were guards less than fifty yards away. The transfer took place in the mid-to-late afternoon when the guards after a heavy two p.m. meal were less vigilant. Ceslav drove one of the factory's trucks up to the entrance. Then, while keeping an eye out for the guards, his friends in the ghetto climbed into the back and took from hiding places inside the cabinets bread, meat, fruit, and vegetables. Ceslav knew he was taking an incredible risk—he would surely be killed if caught—but he refused to let his friends and neighbors in the ghetto starve. "Here is my contribution to fighting the Germans," he would say with a wry smile. Once they were finished, Ceslav and a fellow ghetto worker would deliver the cabinets to their new owners.

Despite his defiance, Ceslav lived in fear that he would be caught. Oftentimes, for recreation, drunken German officers would come at night into the ghetto. Dragging hapless Jews from their families, they would send them running down the narrow streets before shooting them in the back. Ceslav knew that he, too, would be shot if the head of the Gestapo, whom Ceslav saw almost every day, or one of his colleagues spotted him in the ghetto. So he spent many nights hiding in the crawl space beneath his family's room. Shulamith grew to be as distressed as Ceslav. Once casual and outgoing, she was now pensive and withdrawn most days. She worried at night with Ceslav about how long he could maintain his deception. Her mother, meanwhile, had become weak and sick in the ghetto. As for her younger sister, she was losing the childhood she should have enjoyed. Ceslav managed to visit his family in Mława—he would travel there with Doring, who would wait for him before driving them back. Back home, Ceslav would try to comfort Shulamith until they finally fell asleep.

The nights went on like that for months until a knock on the door awoke them at four a.m. one December morning in 1942. It was a Nazi guard telling Ceslav that his boss wanted to see him. Questions raced through Ceslav's mind as he got dressed. Had he been found out? Was he about to be shot? Ceslav followed the guard to the gate where Doring was waiting. His boss took him aside and whispered that in a few hours "a liquidation of the ghetto will start and everyone will be transported out."

"Do you know where to?" Ceslav asked.

Doring replied that he knew nothing else. "I don't know for what purpose," he added. "But I would like to save you from that. Now you will come with me to my place and you will stay with me."

Ceslav replied, "What about my family? What about my wife? What about her sick mother? I cannot leave them. They need my help."

"This is out of the question," Doring said. "I will take you right now, just as you are. You will continue to work for me, just as you did before, and will have a chance to survive."

Ceslav shook his head. In a reply that revealed his essence more than ever before, he said, "Thank you very much, but they need me here," He also thanked Doring for "treating me humanely," and said good-bye. He noticed tears forming in Doring's eyes before he got on the motorcycle that had brought him. Ceslav walked into the ghetto, hoping Doring was wrong.

Two hours later, just before dawn, troops from the German Secret Service arrived in the ghetto, shooting their guns in the air and shouting for everyone to come out into the ghetto plaza. "Out! Out!" they yelled. "Take nothing. Your belongings will be brought to you later." As leashed dogs barked, soldiers kicked open doors ordering those inside to move. Ceslav helped Shulamith support her mother as they stayed one step ahead of the soldiers' swinging clubs. Soon, 4,000 Jews stood jammed in the plaza, their ranks diminished over the previous month through the quiet evacuations of much smaller groups. Ceslav raised his collar and put on dark glasses, fearing that he might be recognized by the commandant or the mayor. "I'll be shot right here if they spot me," he told Shulamith. There wasn't time for anyone to notice Ceslav. Once all the Jews in the ghetto were outside, a German officer announced over a loudspeaker that everyone was being taken to Germany, where they were needed as laborers to aid in the Reich's war effort. Soldiers immediately began herding them through town to the train station several miles away. Because of the condition of Shulamith's mother, Ceslav and his family were allowed to join the elderly on the trucks. Half of the train that Ceslav and his family boarded came from an old luxury passenger train, which had a number of separate, enclosed first-class compartments in each car. Ceslav managed to secure two seats for Shulamith's mother and sister in one of them. He and Shulamith stood beside them, jammed with others beside the curtained glass window of a door that was too obstructed by bodies to close.

At another time, Ceslav might have joked that he had always wanted to ride the Orient Express. But now his mind was filled with dread. In every third car were stationed German troops, ready to shoot to kill if the guard in the observation box atop the last car signaled for the train to stop. It would do so if a passenger had been seen jumping from the moving train in an attempt to escape. None did. After two days and nights, during which few slept and no food or drink was given, Ceslav's train reached its destination. It slowed to a stop shortly after sunset, and Ceslav could hear more than a dozen barking dogs. Looking out the window, the sight of the troops on the platform seemed even more ominous. Suddenly they were shouting, "OUT! OUT!" and bewildered, exhausted families, gripping their suitcases, scrambled from the opened car doors. They stood in bunches until ordered to form a line. "Now we'll know," Ceslav told Shulamith, who leaned closer and closed her eyes. No further words passed before Ceslav and his family were out with the others in line. Ceslav looked up to see an arched, wrought iron sign with each of the capital letters in *ARBEIT MACHT FREI* bound by an iron bar above and below the phrase. It hovered above the entrance to a bevy of red brick buildings. Ceslav knew the phrase meant "WORK

WILL SET YOU FREE," confirming, he hoped, that this was indeed a labor camp.

But suddenly the guards were ordering them not into the red brick buildings but on a march of nearly two miles to a separate camp, Auschwitz-Birkenau, also called Auschwitz II. Ceslav carried most of the suitcases so the sisters could support their mother. Wanting to know where they were, Ceslav asked an elderly man behind him if he knew. He didn't, but the couple behind him said it was Auschwitz. Ceslav still didn't know if there was anything special at Auschwitz. "Men left, women right," ordered troops, driving the crowd apart once they reached the other section. As loved ones separated, some people screamed hysterically. Practically everyone else was crying, including Ceslav. All he knew was that something terrible was happening. And, like the others, fear and panic broke his focus. He couldn't see Shulamith or any of her family. A doctor, a high-ranking officer in the Secret Service squad handling arriving deportees, began separating the women into two sectors. One comprised of younger women and teenage girls; the other of mothers with children, visibly pregnant women, sick and older women.

Only fifty yards separated Ceslav from the women. His eyes raced through the two groups, suddenly stopping at Shulamith's mother among the weaker women. Head bowed as if asleep, she was held up under each arm by Shulamith and Hadassa. Amidst the frigid night air, bright lights, barking dogs, and sobs, they were led into a large brick building. Ceslav never saw them again.

CHAPTER THREE

LIFE IN AUSCHWITZ

The men arriving at Auschwitz from Płońsk were divided into two groups, the same as the women. The old, weak, or sick were sent to one side, and to the other side were the men who were healthy and fit enough for labor. Though Ceslav knew nothing about where either group was headed, he knew that to be sent with the sick, older men would most likely seal his fate. When he was selected as fit for labor, a weight lifted. "Faster! Faster!" shouted the guards as they marched the men in Ceslav's group away. They were disoriented by the bright lights, machine gun–toting guards, and odd-shaped buildings, including several with tall chimneys spewing smoke. Barking dogs helped herd the men into a huge empty building, where they were told to take off their clothes and to deposit their jewelry and valuables on a table. "Anyone retaining anything will be immediately executed," a guard warned. Although the temperature was well below freezing inside the building, the men were forced to sit naked on the cement floor and remain absolutely silent. During the night, several hundred other men from Płońsk joined them shivering on the floor.

Around five o'clock that morning, a group of German soldiers arrived and made the men line up. They were told to stand up, form a line, and file past a table. There, other prisoners who were tattoo artists had needles in hand, tattooing numbers on the undersides of the new prisoners' left forearms. From then on, Ceslav became known as prisoner 84216; his name remaining only in the camp's record book. Soon after, the men were marched to another building, where they were ordered to soak in a foul-smelling disinfectant, followed by a hot shower. As the men emerged from the showers wet and freezing, guards threw white-striped prison clothes at them. Ceslav squeezed into a teenager's pants and jacket. The Dutch wooden shoes he was given were unbearably small. Rather than complain and risk being clubbed to death, as some others had when they asked for better-fitting shoes and clothes, Ceslav kept his silence. He and a group of the men were marched to their new home. The dank former horse stable had holes in the roof and logs nailed together as triple bunk beds for sleeping. The stubs of branches had not been sawed off, so many of the prisoners would have to fit themselves around the equivalent of a spike in order to sleep. A guard said they could eat and rest after they showed how hard they could work. To give them strength, he had urns of coffee brought in, the first sustenance Ceslav had had in three days. Foul as it was, Ceslav drank cup after cup.

About an hour later, Ceslav and the other men in his barrack were taken to a large, open work area. Guards ordered them to run wheelbarrows through dirt paths made muddy from the rain. They then had to fill the barrows with boulders from a rock pile and return the barrow. It was pointless work. Ceslav and the other captives quickly figured out it was actually an endurance test, an exercise meant to separate the strong from the weak. Those taking the endurance test had not been among the lucky ones selected because of a skill they professed, such as machinist or carpenter. If the endurance test did not kill them they would be eligible to perform manual labor in the war production factories of Auschwitz just beyond the perimeter of the camp or work on construction gangs building new barracks, crematoriums, and offices.

Before long, a wooden club slammed the back of Ceslav's head when he failed to load his barrow with enough rocks. After staggering through the mud, he found his feet too weak to move. The guards began hitting everyone in sight, and one after another the men collapsed. Ceslav heard the thud of the clubs and saw the teeth and blood fly. Watching the grim scene, he expected to be beaten to death. The guards for this group of prisoners were especially barbaric because some months earlier, in the spring of 1942, Berlin had ordered commandants in the camp to keep forced laborers alive until they were too weak to work. Not all commandants complied with the new standard operating procedure, however.

Ceslav crawled away from his wheelbarrow and buried himself in the mud so the guards would consider him dead and pass him by. The trick worked. Ten or fifteen minutes later, when the clubbing had ceased, Ceslav ran for the nearest open building. Fortunately, it was a latrine in which he could wash himself off and then sneak back to barrack 19, where the few survivors of the wheelbarrow race had returned. Of the 250 men who had gone out, only about thirty had come back alive. The rest were dragged into the barrack to have their numbers recorded as deceased for the record books. The remaining prisoners had to wash the forearms of the dead so their numbers could be seen. The survivors in barrack 19 were rewarded with a meal of sugary liquid that resembled the gruel fed to farm animals. The guards called it "soup." Ceslav's head was pounding; he was exhausted and starved. So he forced himself to eat. That first week, the prisoners were fed equally disgusting varieties of the so-called soup, plus a small chunk of black bread made partly with sawdust and served with a dollop of margarine. Occasionally a marmalade made from a foul-tasting vegetable, often beet, accompanied the feast.

Ceslav soon noticed that the same prisoners seemed to bully their way ahead of others for their meal each day. One evening he figured out why. If there happened to be some kind of vegetable or remnant of meat at the bottom of the large pot from which the prisoners were served soup, they would purposely knock it over so that its contents spilled on the ground. As the men closest to the soup, they quickly fell to the floor to slobber up the most edible bits, leaving little for their fellow prisoners. While standing in the food line one of those first nights, Ceslav asked the other prisoners what had happened to those on the train not selected for labor. Most of the men shrugged and said they did not know. But then one of the prisoners said, "You will not want to know, but I feel I have to tell you." He proceeded to tell Ceslav about the gas chambers and crematoriums at Auschwitz. The grapevine of rumor and fact was rife. Though he was terrified that Shulamith had been killed, Ceslav kept asking other prisoners if they knew where the women from Płońsk had been taken. A few days later, a prisoner in another block recalled that on the night Ceslav and the Perelmutters had arrived at Auschwitz, he saw an older, sick woman supported by two younger women in the line to the gas chamber. They passed by naked as the *Sonderkommando* work detail of prisoners stood at attention awaiting orders to go in and remove the bodies. It was not known if the prisoner giving Ceslav the news was actually part of the *Sonderkommando* unit or was simply helping Ceslav reach closure. Hearing the news, Ceslav buried his head and hands, rocking back and forth while moaning in anguish. Not only were his wife and in-laws dead, Ceslav had no idea where his father, mother, and sister were.

For Ceslav, the scenes gripping his mind and body were dystopian. It was as if the purgatory he saw arriving at Auschwitz had turned into the horrors of hell. Smoke from incinerated bodies, flames, stench, and screams were constant. Grim-faced old men and frightened mothers and children shuffled cluelessly down the road leading to crematoria 111 and nearby (burning) pits. The rabid laughter of the SS and heartbreaking screams reached into the night. During the day Ceslav and fellow prisoners were hopeless, moving like shadows from work detail to work detail.[1]

Auschwitz had not initially been designed as a death factory. After occupying Poland, the Reich planned a major development project of new farms, foundries, mines, and factories in a twenty-three-square-mile region of the country. For this complex, the Germans chose Auschwitz (Oświęcim), a 500-year-old town of 12,000 inhabitants, for its existing railway junction linking Berlin, Vienna, Warsaw, and other hubs. The original camp, Auschwitz I, was established on the grounds of a former Polish army base in the spring of 1940 with twenty-two brick buildings for political and criminal prisoners in a space that was a little over 200 yards by 300 yards. The SS leadership then built a much-larger second camp (1,750 yards by 550 yards), two miles away near the village of Brzezinka (Birkenau) known as Auschwitz II (a.k.a. Auschwitz-Birkenau). And in late January 1942, Reichsführer-SS Heinrich Himmler established in Berlin the Reich Security Main Office, led by SS General Reinhard Heydrich. As head of the *Einsatzgruppen* Security Police and Service in the early years of the war, he had overseen the brutal murder by gunshot and experimental gas chamber wagons of one million people in Poland and the Soviet Union. On January 20, 1942, Heydrich convened a conference at Wannsee, a suburb of Berlin, euphemistically entitling the agenda "Desires and Ideas of the Foreign Office in Connection with the Intended Total Solution of the Jewish Question in Europe."[2]

The "total solution" referred to in the agenda called for the annihilation of eleven million European Jews, listed country by country, including 330,000 from England and five million from the Soviet Union. Thus, Auschwitz-Birkenau became a killing center for Jews unable to work and a concentration camp for those chosen to work. Many of the prisoners chosen for work were forced to assist their captors in the gruesome tasks of collecting the discarded clothes of victims and taking their bodies from the gas chambers to the furnaces to be incinerated.

During 1943, Germany increased the number of gas chambers from two to four. A year later, as the crematoriums could not keep up with the number of corpses from the gas chambers, the Jewish *Sonderkommando* work units were ordered to dig huge pits for fires to do the job.

"You know, what was decisive was not the year 1933 [when Hitler and the Nazi Party came to power]," said famed writer-philosopher Hannah Arendt, a German Jewish refugee who escaped via France to the United States in 1940. "What was decisive was the day we learned about Auschwitz.... At first, we didn't believe it...because militarily it was unnecessary and uncalled for," she added.[3] Her most famous work, the book *The Origins of Totalitarianism*, stemmed from essays she wrote in 1944 in which she noted that the camps "are the laboratories where changes in human nature are tested" and "total domination of the human spirit is proved to be attainable." She referred to such domination as "radical evil," a noteworthy phrase she made even more memorable when she wrote *Eichmann in Jerusalem: A Report on the Banality of Evil*, following her reporting on the war trial of Adolf Eichmann.

These vivid scenes of Auschwitz deepened Ceslav's depression during his first few months there, while he continued to be sent out to the work areas every day for unproductive tasks such as building a shed one day and tearing it down the next. Conditions at the camp, such as the meager helpings of food, compounded the gruesome environment even further. He had to walk around barefoot in the frigid weather; his small wooden shoes tucked under his arms or placed nearby in case a guard questioned their whereabouts. In just eight weeks, he was down to eighty-eight pounds, half of what he weighed when he arrived at Auschwitz in December 1942. He had lost nearly all his physical strength, and at times, most of his will to live. Thoughts of death and the urge to fall asleep forever were inescapable. Even so, Ceslav was holding up better than many of his fellow prisoners. In his barrack one day in February 1943, he recognized a man he had gone to school with in Mława. Ceslav was several grades behind the other man, whose name was Bucio. Exhausted and barely able to walk, he asked Ceslav to help him stand up when the guards came in for inspection. "I can't go on," he whispered from his bunk as Ceslav stood beside him. "If they see I'm ill, I'll be taken out and shot." Ceslav agreed to help. Bucio was the administrative clerk to Janus, the "block elder." The SS chose their elders from among the prisoners, making them responsible for the smooth operations of the barracks. Oftentimes the elders, also known as *kapos*, were criminals from the jails in Poland and could be counted on to apply discipline.

One night, after seeing Bucio being helped by Ceslav, Janus pulled him aside. "How good are you at mathematics?" he asked. Ceslav told him he graduated at the top of his high school class. Nodding with satisfaction, Janus asked in German, "Do you speak German?" "*Fließend*," Ceslav replied, using the German word for "fluently." Janus said he doubted Bucio was going to survive and that in a few months all the prisoners from barrack 19 would move to a newly constructed part of the camp. "When we are moved you can be my clerk. Do you want the job?" Since it meant more security and avoiding the useless and dangerous work outside the barracks, Ceslav immediately said yes. For now, he remained on a work detail, but he would be protected by Janus, who had influence with the guards. Janus also arranged to get Ceslav better-fitting clothes and shoes. The suit he received was drab chalk-gray, not black and white striped like the one he'd worn before. I've been promoted, thought Ceslav as he put on the shabby outfit. It was the first sign since his arrival that his sense of humor hadn't left him.

Around the same time, Ceslav received news that filled him with hope. He learned from Bucio that his father, Herman, was still alive and in Auschwitz. The only problem was he was housed in a barrack about 200 yards away. If Ceslav tried to visit him, the guards would most likely kill him for venturing outside his designated work area. One afternoon he decided to risk it anyway. As he approached Herman's barrack, Ceslav asked one of the prisoners for assistance in pointing out his father. The man warned Ceslav that a reunion at that time would be too dangerous, as the guards would surely spot him as an outsider. "Go back to your barrack," the other prisoner said. "We will find a reason to bring him to you." The next day Ceslav looked up from his bunk to find his father approaching him, accompanied by another man. He had not seen his father since Shulamith and he were married in Mława. The other man with Herman was David Shmulewski, a deputy elder who had known his father as a young man in Koło, a town in central Poland. After embracing and brushing away tears from each other's face, Ceslav and his father shared what they knew of their family. He informed Ceslav that his mother and sister had met the same fate as Shulamith in the gas chamber. As the two men quietly cried, Shmulewski touched Ceslav's arm.

"I know your family from Koło," he said. "They were good people. Is there anything I can do for you?" Ceslav replied, "Please do everything to keep my father alive." Before his father left, Ceslav broke off a piece of bread from his pocket and gave it to him. In turn, Herman reached in his pocket for a piece of the precious bread he, too, had salvaged and gave it to Ceslav. The two parted on that symbolic act. Several days later, Ceslav found the chance to sneak off to his father's barracks to inquire about him. When Ceslav saw Shmulewski, the vice elder shook his head. He said his father had been in the block that morning but then had gone out for a walk and had not come back. Ceslav knew what that meant. He thanked Shmulewski for his nice words a few days earlier and returned to his barrack, miserable and abandoned. Now he truly was alone in the world.

Over the next few months, Ceslav struggled against despair. Every morning he went out to work, without breakfast, gritting his teeth as a 120-member brass band of prisoners played marching songs at the gate of the barbed wire enclosure, which separated the barracks from the work area. On the prisoners' return in the late afternoon, another band would greet them with show tunes or a poorly executed version of Beethoven's Fifth Symphony. Some of the work seemed to have no purpose other than to keep them busy until needed in the factories adjoining the camp. Groups of laborers would construct small buildings one day, only to tear them down the next. Or they would haul gravel and sand back and forth for no apparent reason. By midafternoon, drunken SS officers would take delight in clubbing prisoners or using them for target practice. Many mornings as he went out to work, Ceslav feared he wouldn't make it back to the barrack alive that night.

Then, several months later, Ceslav's job changed. He and other men in his barrack moved to a new barrack. Made of wood and built like a stable, it could fit up to 1,000 men, versus several hundred in the smaller barrack. Otherwise, it looked the same: long and narrow, with the same primitive bunks. Ceslav became the administrative clerk for the new barrack, replacing Bucio, who had been taken out and shot after he'd been deemed too sick to work. This meant Ceslav no longer had to join the work detail each day. His job now was to keep tabs on the hundreds of prisoners housed in his barrack. That summer, Jews from Greece filled the places of the dead from Ceslav's barrack. So many arrived thin and sickly from their trip that veteran prisoners in the barrack referred to them as "candidates" for the gas chambers. For some reason, the Greeks had not gone through the typical selection process that had sent so many others immediately to their deaths. But everyone knew their time was coming. The plight of these "candidates" was even worse than that of most of the other European prisoners, as no one in the camp spoke Greek. Ceslav saw the confused and disbelieving looks on their faces. Some turned to him with gestures seeking help, apparently because he showed more patience than his peers. Huddled in the barrack, the Greek prisoners were an appalling sight—many had already wasted to skin and bones. One day an SS doctor named Thilo came to the barrack to thin out the ranks. He chose about 300 of the nearly 1,000 men in the barrack, almost all of whom were the so-called candidates. Guards called out their tattooed numbers to Ceslav, who pulled their cards from his file. While the men waited at the barrack, Ceslav took the cards to the head office. Trucks would arrive a few hours later and guards would call the numbers as supplied from the central office.

Knowing that this was the routine, Ceslav tried to buy time for some of the candidates to regain their strength. As he walked the few hundred yards to the central office with the cards in his hand, he took about eighty of the cards and placed them inside his shirt. He turned over the remainder at the office. Back at the barrack, Ceslav's elder, a Polish criminal named Alfred Zabielski, asked him how many men were to be taken. Hearing the number 220, Zabielski shouted, "That's not possible! The doctor selected many more than that." Suspecting what had happened, Zabielski said he would turn Ceslav in to the SS. "I'm not going to the gas chambers for what you did," added Zabielski. Ceslav suggested they take their argument outside the barrack and led the way to the rear exit. Eight feet from the door there was an electrified 780-volt fence, far more energy than needed to kill on contact. Ceslav grabbed the taller and stronger Zabielski by the collar and spun him toward the wire fence, where hundreds of inmates had died, either in vain attempts to escape or simply to commit suicide. Ceslav issued an ultimatum. "Both of us can be finished on the fence," he said, "or you can keep quiet." Before Zabielski could answer, a siren sounded and loudspeakers told camp elders to report to the central office. Ceslav returned to his desk in the barrack and slid the cards he had inside his shirt back into his file. Without any evidence of Ceslav's deception, Zabielski had no choice but to go along with the scheme, which went undetected. Several hours later the trucks arrived and took away 220 prisoners. Ceslav looked at some of the eighty left behind and thought, At least now they have a chance.

The small victory did little to buoy Ceslav's spirits. Drained by the loss of Shulamith and the rest of his family, and desperate for food, Ceslav barely had enough strength to stay alive. Ceslav was not alone in his despair. Just in his own barrack, there were hundreds of men in the same condition—their personalities seemingly gone, blank expressions on their faces, and virtually no energy in their bodies. Day after day, SS guards selected the weakest of the men and sent them to the gas chambers. If that was to be his fate, Ceslav thought in one of his more lucid moments, at least he would die in the same way that Shulamith had. He even would prefer it to being clubbed or shot to death by the guards.

Every day he filled out lengthy reports—all by number, not by name—on who went to the infirmary and which prisoners were either out on work detail or had been taken to the crematorium. Around five to ten prisoners from his barrack died each night. Ceslav dutifully walked to the central administrative station with reports of the dead. It was on one of those walks that Ceslav recalled the dying breaths and moaning he had heard from men in his barrack the night before. He sighed and stopped abruptly. He felt he could not go on. He did not scream, Job-like, at the heavens, "Why God, why?" Nor did he lash out at the next Nazi he saw. Instead, he wondered, What would have become of those men if they had survived Auschwitz and gone back to their everyday lives? In that moment, Ceslav chose life—not only for himself, but to give other prisoners, like the Greeks, a chance to live as well. This madness had to end. "Somehow I will find a miracle to get out of here," Ceslav told himself. "I do not know how or who is going to help. But I must get out."

CHAPTER FOUR

PLANNING AN ESCAPE

One frigid morning the previous winter, Ceslav came upon a man sitting atop a frozen dead body, using it as a bench. He was warming an aluminum pot of coffee over a small fire. "Would you like some coffee?" he asked. Behind him was an open shed crammed with bodies of fellow inmates who had died the night before. Ceslav nodded. The man's name was Alfred "Fredo" Wetzler, the clerk for barrack 9. The two inmates were both from residential section D, one of five compounds composed of thirty-two or so barracks or "blocks," as they also were known. Alfred was waiting for a truck to take the dead bodies from his block to the crematorium. Ceslav and Alfred were chatting when the trucks arrived. Ceslav watched as the SS guard on the truck checked the numbers on the dead men's arms three times with Alfred. The contrast of the SS's careless disregard for life while insisting upon such fastidious detail was detestable to Ceslav and Alfred. At the headcount each morning, every prisoner had to be there—the living and those who died during the night. Strangely, there was no accounting made of the thousands of people who died in the gas chambers. But if one of the prisoners was not counted, there was a problem. An unaccounted-for prisoner meant a possible escape. And then the world might learn the awful truth of what took place at the camps. "There's a method to their madness," Alfred wryly commented.

Thus began Ceslav's friendship with Alfred. Both were twenty-two years old, and they would come to share the hope of escaping what they referred to as Dante's hell. They also shared compassion for their fellow prisoners. Ceslav came to appreciate Alfred as someone who maintained his manhood, dignity, and decency despite all that was going on around him. They shared any information they had about new arrivals and their fate. The only hint Ceslav ever had about Alfred meaning to make use of what he knew about the camp was an offhand comment he made one day: "Someone has to tell the world about this!" Ceslav had long shared that view without ever having discussed it with Alfred.

Even if they or someone else could tell the world, would the Allies take action to stop the massacre? Britain and the US were battling Japan in the Western Pacific while the Soviet Union was battling Germany and Italy in Europe. Allied intelligence was well aware of the death camps and would only go so far as to threaten Germany about the Holocaust. Fortunately, in 1943, the tides of war were going against the Axis powers, forcing retreat on all strategic fronts. In 1944, the Western Allies freed France, the Soviet Union advanced toward Germany, and Japan was on its heels. But that wasn't enough for the US and Britain to add saving the Jews to their military campaign. And while Germany was losing the military war, it was determined to see its hatred of the Jews through to victory.

Escaping Auschwitz was against the odds. Of the more than 800 attempts (150 of which were by Jews) registered by the camp from 1940–1945, only 127 were deemed successful.[1] The multi-acre work area outside the residential encampment was not encircled with an electrified fence, but rather secured with a high wooden watchtower stationed every eighty meters. The guards remained on duty throughout the day and would shoot to kill anyone who approached within ten meters of this outer border, as the large sentry chain was known. Many of the would-be escapees were *Auf der Flucht erschossen*, shot on the run. The watchtowers were left unmanned once all prisoners had been accounted for upon their return to the electrified barbed wire residential encampment. Here, ten-meter-high guard towers stationed every fifty meters served as the inner perimeter sentry chain. If a prisoner was unaccounted for at the gate check-in to the barrack compounds, not only were the guards left on duty in the work area but also search parties of SS troops and trained Alsatian dogs scoured the grounds. Such searches typically lasted three days before the missing were either captured or declared escaped. After that, the watch towers were again left unmanned throughout the night.

Outside the work area's outer perimeter sentry chain was a forty-square kilometer control "zone" between the Sola and Vistula Rivers. The SS had evacuated most of the Polish population in the area, replacing them with German citizens who would report suspected escapees. Most of them were found within a few day and were either shot or hanged. One captured inmate in late 1943 was hanged in the camp's kitchen, where prisoner representatives came for buckets of food to take back to their barracks. Upon entering the kitchen, they saw him hanging with a sign around his neck that said in German, "Hurrah, Hurrah. I escaped and now I am back." Another time, ten prisoners were punished for the successful escape of a man in their barrack. Since it was December, they were hung by their feet upside down in the form of a Hanukkah menorah, then doused with oil and set afire while the guards sang Christmas carols. When the sirens signaling an escape sounded early on the afternoon of April 7, Ceslav did not know it was for Alfred. His friend had never confided in him that he planned to escape Auschwitz. It wasn't until that evening that Ceslav learned Alfred was one of the two escapees. The other was Walter Rosenberg, a fellow clerk who later took the name Rudolf Vrba. As clerks, Wetzler and Rosenberg were more worrisome to the SS than other less informed escapees. They knew too much about the inner workings of the camp.

In the aftermath of the escape, all of Auschwitz's eight Jewish clerks, including Ceslav, were forced to report to the camp commandant. They would be punished for their fellow clerks' escape. This included a demotion from clerk to work detail. There also was concern about a potential conspiracy plot among the clerks, so they were tortured to admit whatever they knew about the plan. Each of them had to step forward, lower his pants, bend over a table, and step into a foot stirrup that locked. An SS guard then took a wooden club and stuck each clerk twenty-five times on their bare backsides. Ceslav denied a conspiracy and passed out from the torture, as did the others. He came to when someone threw a bucket of cold water on his head. Fellow prisoners then helped him back to his newly assigned barrack 18, where he was ordered to see a new kapo named Adam Rozycki. A block elder of another barrack who managed a group of prisoners in the labor details, Rozycki was the one kapo Ceslav dreaded. When the Germans had emptied Poland's prisons into Auschwitz in June 1940, Rozycki offered to help keep other prisoners in line. A convicted killer, he quickly won the respect of the camp's SS guards, first by brutally murdering dozens of his fellow inmates, then by opening up a smuggling pipeline that brought in vodka, bacon, cheeses, and other delicacies. A hulking, bald-headed man of about fifty years of age, Rozycki could do practically anything he wanted. This included taking delight in strangling cowering Jews whose only offense was failing to lift their caps in homage. There was talk he even had a mistress who came and went through Auschwitz's gates at will.

What does that sadist want with me? thought Ceslav. *I've stayed alive here for this long by staying away from his kind.* He queried other prisoners about Rozycki. The odd thing, they told Ceslav, was that, from all appearances, Rozycki had changed from the previous years. "They're now calling him the angel of Auschwitz," one of Ceslav's bunkmates said. Though he was no less mean looking, an image burnished by his wooden leg and sneering smile, Rozycki recently had begun treating his latest clerk with leniency, even respect. Other prisoners gathered around as Ceslav continued asking about Rozycki. They told him that Rozycki gave preferential treatment to former Polish judges, politicians, and professors, and that he protected them when they went out on work detail. Maybe, as the cell block rumor mill had it, Rozycki had heard reports that Germany was losing the war, and he feared being found out as someone who had conspired with the Nazis. "Come in. Sit down. Would you like some vodka? Coffee?" Rozycki told Ceslav when he arrived at Rozycki's office, cap in hand. The office was actually a shack that served as the assembly point and equipment storage for Rozycki's workforce of fifty men. It was about one hundred yards beyond the barbed wire fences and gates that enclosed row after row of single story bunkhouses. Rozycki was sitting in the shack's work area, eating a slice of cooked bacon. Accepting the coffee, Ceslav drew in his breath and said, "You wanted to see me?" "Yes," Rozycki said, taking Ceslav by the arm outside. "The usual way Jews like you leave this place is through the chimneys," pointing toward the crematoriums about a half mile away. Cryptically, he added, "Let me know if there is any way I can help you."

Rozycki went on to note that he had heard Ceslav was one of the camp's most clever prisoners, and that he had mastered the system as well as anyone. "You have everything but the bacon," he laughed, holding his delicacy aloft. "That is why I made sure to have you assigned to my workforce." Ceslav wondered what that implied. But before he had the chance to ask, Rozycki told him to rejoin the work detail. The day then went smoothly as workers in Rozycki's group methodically, and with a certain amount of pride in their work, built, tore down, and rebuilt a small shelter. Is it a trick? Ceslav wondered that evening as he tossed from side to side, unable to sleep. Maybe Rozycki just wanted to show the SS he had foiled an escape plan. There was a premium now on such information. Escapes meant that the secret, of which Auschwitz was not a labor camp but a killing factory, would become known far and wide. The young Pole didn't know how much the Allies knew about the vast Auschwitz-Birkenau complex. But certainly testimony from eyewitnesses would cause outrage from the more civilized world, he thought. Is this the chance I've been waiting for? Ceslav mused. He had heard about the underground bunker in the work area that his friend Wetzler had used to escape and wondered if something similar in another part of the work area might aid in his escape as well. He had no alternative but to trust Rozycki. Here was someone in power seemingly offering to help him escape.

"Adam, I want to escape from here," was how Ceslav greeted his kapo the next morning. "But what kind of plan do you have?" Rozycki replied. Ceslav explained his plan to create a hideout in the camp that could serve as a bunker for him and a fellow escapee, and how he hoped two men from the work detail would help him build and camouflage it. "Fine, but I want to be your partner," said Rozycki, catching Ceslav completely off guard. His mind raced. Rozycki's wooden leg would slow Ceslav down. And how could Ceslav know that once out in the open, Rozycki might not turn on him to eliminate his last connection to Auschwitz? Though half his age, Ceslav knew he was no match for Rozycki's strength. But how could he refuse his request? Or do so without incurring his wrath? "I beg your pardon, but please don't get insulted," Ceslav replied. "But have you taken into consideration your wooden leg and that you are likely to be recognized within ten kilometers?" Ceslav had a point. Rozycki knew that local residents would be on the lookout for escapees, ready to turn them in rather than risk retribution from the SS. He agreed with Ceslav's reasoning but added, "I will have to approve your partner." Ceslav breathed a sigh of relief and quickly suggested the only other person to whom he had ever revealed his escape plan: Josef Borenstein, a good friend of Ceslav from Płońsk who had been with him on the train to Auschwitz. But several days after they had agreed to the plan, Borenstein was transferred to the crematorium work detail and the two lost contact. "You had better come up with someone else fast," Rozycki told Ceslav. "I'll be put in charge of a new commando [detachment] of prisoners in a few weeks and you'll be on your own after that." Ceslav's choices were limited. He needed someone who was physically strong enough to survive not only the ordeal in the hideout but also probably several weeks of travel by foot through occupied Poland to reach safety. Most of all, his partner had to have courage and an extraordinary will to live.

Ceslav then thought of Arnost Rosin, who worked as a clerk in Ceslav's former barrack. He held the position because he could speak Hungarian, Slovakian, and German. Before the war, Arnost had lived in Slovakia where he sold mechanical equipment and automobiles throughout those countries. Like Ceslav, Arnost was a clerk recording the life and death of his barrack mates before he was named the kapo elder in charge of the barrack. Wetzler had become his clerk. As a consequence, Arnost had come under scrutiny following Wetzler's escape.

Ceslav liked that Arnost rebuffed the two SS men who had interrogated him. When they put a gun to his head demanding that he talk, Arnost told them to go ahead and shoot—he was going to die in Auschwitz anyway. The bunkhouse sector where Rosin resided was on the other side of the Birkenau camp from Ceslav. Even if he agreed to the plan, he would not have the chance to help prepare the hideout, which was in Ceslav's part of the camp. When Ceslav raised this with Rozycki, the kapo said he would let Rosin join on one condition: He had to convince Ceslav he would be able to find his way to the hideout at the given time without raising suspicion. Just before leaving to visit Rosin, Ceslav asked Rozycki, "Adam, you are taking a big risk getting involved with this. Why are you being so kind?" By this time, Ceslav's suspicion of Rozycki had vanished, and he had come to think of him as the only friend he had left at Auschwitz. Rozycki paused, seemingly unsure of what he was about to say. Then, in an uncharacteristically soft, shaky voice, he told Ceslav of an incident several months earlier.

"I was going from barrack to barrack one morning, grabbing prisoners for a special assignment some of the guards had lined up. They were going to make the men race against each other carrying sacks of rocks. The guards had even laid out an obstacle course. I knew they would be drinking and making bets. And if the prisoner a guard chose to bet on lost the race, he would be shot at the finish line." The kapo then shook his head, as if to say even he had had enough of such brutality. What convinced him to end his role in the carnage, he said, was when he came upon an aged Jewish man praying by the side of his bunk. "I laughed and said, 'Ok, old man, your prayers are answered. I won't make you go out [on work detail] this time.' The man looked up and said, 'That's not what I am praying for.'" Rozycki asked him what else he could want. "He replied, 'I was thanking God.' Naturally, that made me even more curious, so I asked him what there was to thank him for here." Tears began filling Rozycki's eyes as he recalled what the Jewish man said next. "He looked up and said simply, 'I am thanking him for not making me like them.'"

Leaving Rozycki, Ceslav sought out Rosin in his barrack. "May I see you outside?" Ceslav said, motioning to the door. They walked behind the barrack a few feet away from the electrified fence. Ceslav got right to the point. "I have a plan for an escape that will work if the right person is my partner. I think you are that person." Arnost said he was interested but wanted to think about it overnight. "The kapo of my work detail will come by tomorrow to help you understand what will happen and to find out your answer," Ceslav said. When Rozycki stopped by the following day, he took Arnost for a walk to the labor sector. There, he led him past the quarry, where the bunker hideout was already being built by some men in Rozycki's work group. They walked farther along and came upon Ceslav. As the three men spoke about the plan, Arnost made his decision to join Ceslav. Like Ceslav, he had survived at Auschwitz for at least a year and a half. It was doubtful either of them could last another two years. "I'm thirty years old," Arnost said. "I want to live a few more years." Ceslav knew that escaping now, following the successful flight of Alfred and Walter, would be even more difficult than before. To make sure that didn't happen again, the SS had doubled the number of guards in the work area. Fortunately, the area was vast enough for Ceslav and Arnost to find a likely hiding place at the bottom of a two-story-high gravel quarry several hundred yards away from the outer boundary line. There, he and Arnost would hide out for three days and nights after being discovered missing. That's how long the SS searched for escaped prisoners in the work area before assuming they had already gotten beyond the perimeter. In addition to the bunker, the two would need supplies. A friend of Ceslav from Płońsk, who supervised the collections of clothes from the dead, provided them with two pairs of electrician's coveralls, boots, and a watch for both Ceslav and his partner. They would need the watch to know when to leave the bunker and the clothing to avoid detection on the outside. Ceslav also needed turpentine to soak the ground above his planned hiding place to keep the trained dogs from sniffing them out. He obtained the turpentine from another prisoner in the painter's work group after saying it was needed for a project.

To build the hideout bunker, Rozycki convinced two Polish prisoners to help Ceslav in order to use the bunker to escape after them. While one stood watch at the top of the twenty-foot-deep sloping quarry, Ceslav and the other dug a grave-like hole in the mound sloping out of the quarry wall. During the week before the escape, Ceslav slept only a total of ten hours. Throughout the night, the tension of digging the bunker little by little without coming under suspicion as SS troops patrolled at random left him on edge. Finally, it was done. Two persons could lie horizontally in it with a one-inch diameter pipe stretching through the wood and dirt roof to let in air. The roof was supported by wooden posts at the head and foot of the makeshift grave. On the morning of the planned escape, Ceslav met with Rozycki at his construction shack in the work yard to say farewell and to thank him. He drank coffee, having turned down Rozycki's offer of vodka to keep his head clear for what lay ahead. "Take this," Rozycki said, holding out a bag of diamonds and a gold watch as a farewell present. "Thank you. But they will torture and kill us more cruelly if we are captured with valuables taken from the camp," said Ceslav, embracing the much taller man. Rozycki asked what the pair will do if something goes wrong with their plan. "Whatever happens," Ceslav said, "it can't be worse than staying here."

CHAPTER FIVE

HITLER vs. HORTHY

Throughout the spring of 1944, as Ceslav planned his escape, he was increasingly motivated by more than his own survival. New gas chambers and crematoriums were under construction at Auschwitz, which would allow the Germans to kill even more prisoners more quickly. A new rail line also was being built inside the camp, rumored to be in preparation for the arrival of hundreds of thousands of Jews from Hungary. One of the Reich's top officials, Reichsführer-SS Heinrich Himmler, had even visited the camp that spring to check on the status of the project. Someone had to tell the world what was happening at Auschwitz. Alfred Wetzler, Ceslav's friend, and Walter Rosenberg, who had escaped on April 7, might be dead for all he knew. As Ceslav showed up for work in Rozycki's labor detail one morning in early May, he was about 110 yards away from the barbed wire fence bordering the new railway line. Ceslav put down his shovel and watched the train come to a halt on the new ramp, each of its forty sealed boxcars crammed with up to one hundred people. When SS guards slid the carriage car doors open, bedraggled deportees staggered onto the ramp, confused and bewildered. Powerless, they took directions to fall into one line or the other. He counted that one in six were directed to the shorter line, knowing the rest would be gassed. Ceslav turned away when he heard the anguished cries of families being separated. He learned later that evening that the train contained mostly political prisoners and their families from Hungary. Two weeks later, on May 15 and 16, convoys of Jews from the provinces of Hungary began arriving on a mostly daily basis.

At the same time in Budapest, SS-Obersturmbannführer Adolf Eichmann was coordinating with the Hungarian Ministry of the Interior and the Hungarian gendarmerie the dispatch of trainload after trainload of frightened Jewish men, women, and children into German custody at the Hungarian border and then on to Auschwitz. Although orders for deportations were planned much higher up than Eichmann, he had a grandiose vision of himself as the annihilator of the Jews. A workaholic, splitting his time between a Gestapo office building in Berlin and visits to ghettos and RSHA transit camps for Jews in occupied countries, he reportedly referred to himself as the "bloodhound" and bragged he "would achieve formidable results in the briefest possible time."[1] In reality, Eichmann inflated his power quite freely and after the war his role had been greatly exaggerated both in popular and some scholarly work, said Peter Black, who tracked down Nazi war criminals for the US Department of Justice and was chief historian of the

US Holocaust Memorial Museum from 1997 to 2016. He added that of the roughly six million Jews killed in German-occupied or -influenced Europe during World War II, Eichmann played a role in the deportation and murder of just 16 percent. Outside of Poland, western USSR, former Yugoslavia, Germany, and Holland, the Nazi goal of eradicating Jews in other countries had not been overly successful. More than half of the Jews in France and Italy survived the war.[2]

On March 12, 1944, Eichmann summoned to his Berlin residence SS officials, many of whom had coordinated previous deportation operations. He informed them that Germany was about to invade Hungary, whose leaders had been making overtures to join the Allies. As a side benefit of occupying Hungary, the Germans also intended to extract from the country more than 700,000 Jews, of whom the Germans hoped to deploy 200,000 as forced laborers in Auschwitz and other concentration camps. It would be the Reich's largest deportation operation to a single location of the war.

Although Ceslav had never set foot in Hungary, his sympathy for the plight of so many of its people, his fellow Jews, would join him to the country's history. Hungary at the time was the most assimilated country in Eastern Europe. There were Jewish industrial leaders, bankers, doctors, journalists, writers, artists, and even sports stars. A wealthy Jewish family, the Weiss family, owned the Manfred Weiss Works, one of the largest arms manufacturers in Europe. The rapid integration of Jews into Hungarian society began in the second half of the nineteenth century. The Magyar party, composed of wealthy Christian landowners and impoverished nobles, needed Hungary's Jews to sign on to the party to keep control. For the Jews, adopting the country's Magyar language allowed them to play important roles in commerce and other emerging lucrative professions. Within a few decades, Hungarian Jews had launched and were running most of the country's major banks and heavy industries and were playing major roles in art, sports, and literature.[3] Assimilated Jews joined their Hungarian peers in fashionable dress at the promenade that took place each weekend in Budapest along the Corso, the boardwalk on the Pest side of the Danube River. For Hungary's Jews, the period in the late nineteenth and early twentieth centuries became known as their "Golden Era."

The country's leader since 1920 was Miklós Horthy, a suave, not-very-bright, silver-haired aristocrat who was conscious of his image as "His Serene Highness the Regent of the Kingdom of Hungary." He had been commander in chief of the Austro-Hungarian Navy in the last year of World War I, and at public ceremonies he would wear all his medals with his naval uniform. Horthy was a fervent nationalist. In 1939, the then-seventy-two-year-old Horthy physically attacked a group of fascists who staged a protest at a performance at the Budapest opera house. Horthy jumped from his seat to confront the men, members of the Arrow Cross Party. In the ensuing brawl, Horthy tackled one of them to the ground, slapped his face, and shouted, "So you would betray your country, would you?"[4] Horthy's brand of nationalism was anathema to Hitler. In the late 1930s, tensions began to surface between the two countries. It started with a state visit in the summer of 1938 to Germany by Horthy and his wife, Magdolna. Hitler had invited the Horthys

Miklós Horthy (left) with Adolf Hitler en route to contentious state visit by Horthy in 1938.

to the launching of the *Prinz Eugen*, a new German naval vessel, which Magdolna was to christen. Horthy, the former Admiral, relished the opportunity.

After the christening, Hitler took the Horthys on his private ship to review Germany's naval fleet on the Baltic Sea. On the trip back to Berlin by train for the evening's festivities, Hitler asked for a tête-à-tête with Horthy at his office in Berlin. Hungary was not yet an ally, so Horthy expected Hitler to make a strategic overture. He was right. As the two sat down for their meeting that afternoon, Hitler spelled out his grand ambition for conquering all of Europe. He wanted Hungary to help by marching its troops into Slovakia from the south while Germany invaded its neighbor Czechoslovakia from the west.[5] Horthy refused. "The friendly mood of the morning had evaporated; our conversation ended on a rather unpleasant note,"

Horthy recalled later.[6] At the same time, a meeting between Hitler's officials and the Hungarian leaders who had accompanied Horthy ended with Germany's foreign minister, Joachim von Ribbentrop, stating, "If you want to join in the meal, you must help with the cooking."[7] What von Ribbentrop meant was that if Hungary wanted to take back territory it had lost in World War 1, it had to join the Axis alliance. Germany went ahead and invaded Czechoslovakia without Hungary's help. The Reich, nonetheless, kept pursuing Hungary by gifting it southeastern Czechoslovakia—territory Hungary had controlled before the war. So Hungary joined the Nazi alliance in December 1938, hoping for more repatriations. Horthy celebrated his Czech present by riding in full naval attire on his white horse at the head of his troops into Kassa (present day Košice), a former Czech city about 140 miles northeast of Budapest. In April 1939, Horthy proved his allegiance to the Reich. He withdrew his country from the League of Nations, which led American journalists to label Hungary "the jackal of Europe."[8] Throughout 1939 and 1940, Hungary continued to recover lost territory with the support of the Axis powers, expanding Hungary's Jewish population from 450,000 to more than 725,000. Horthy, who earlier had told his prime minister he had been "an anti-Semite throughout my life,"[9] resisted pressure from Germany to deport Hungary's Jews. He continued to maintain that without them, the country's economy would collapse. But on March 12, 1943, at a reception for Hungarian minister Bela Lukacs at the German legation in Budapest, a plan was set for Hitler's private secretary Martin Bormann to inform Lukacs that Germany expected Hungary to fall in line with other countries in dealing harshly with "the Jewish question." Horthy was then invited to visit Berlin a month later to discuss the matter with Hitler. There, the Führer told Horthy bluntly that Jews "were to be treated like T.B. bacilli, which were dangerous to a healthy organism."[10] Horthy, once again, turned a deaf ear to Hitler's demands.

From Hitler's perspective, harsher moves against Hungary were needed. Germany sent Edmund Veesenmayer, a brigadier general in the SS, to Hungary to prepare the way for a German occupation. In a memorandum to Nazi leadership following his visit, Veesenmayer wrote that Jews in Hungary are saboteurs, helping "as many—if not twice as many—Hungarians... realize a fantastically large-scale plan of sabotage and spying" against Germany. He then suggested that Horthy would "accept without resistance any [new] Prime Minister the Führer demands...if only to save himself and his dynasty and not to bury his dreams of being a Duke before he dies."[11] As it happened, Horthy was already devising a plan to fend off Hitler and a potential invasion. By the start of 1944, the Hungarian leader knew that the Axis was losing the war and the Red Army was marshaling forces at Hungary's eastern border. After putting out feelers to the Allies, along with the Soviet Union, he had his minister president, Miklós Kállay, offer to surrender once Russian troops entered Hungary. But Germany knew of Kállay's secret overture to the Allies, thanks to Veesenmayer's contacts in Horthy's ministry.

In mid-March 1944, the Führer again summoned Horthy to Berlin—purportedly to discuss Hungary's role in the war. In a private meeting in Hitler's study, Horthy found Hitler "ill at ease." He started by saying he knew of Kállay's overtures to the Allies. Referring to Italy's surrender to the Allies the previous September, Hitler said he had to take "precautionary measures" to ensure something similar didn't happen with Hungary. Horthy fired back that if that meant sending occupying forces, the Hungarian people would greet German troops with outrage. Hitler began ranting, and Horthy abruptly walked out.[12] Before Horthy could leave Berlin, an air alarm went off. Telephone lines were cut, and Horthy was asked to resume his conversation with Hitler over lunch. Hitler "picked nervously at his vegetarian food" in the elaborate dining hall. Afterwards, Hitler tried to smooth things over by saying he would try to stop the invasion. He called in Field Marshal Wilhelm Keitel, who replied that it was too late, the troops were already on the march.[13] With nothing left to argue, Horthy announced he would step down as regent. But Hitler, a stickler for legality, even of his making, clearly wanted an acquiescent leader to stay on to ensure the occupation would not spark a revolution in Hungary. He wooed him with a pledge to withdraw German troops once Horthy appointed a new government to Hitler's liking. But Hungary had to accept a German occupation and deliver 300,000 Jewish workers to the Reich, or else it would lose the territories it had received from Germany. Horthy is said to have agreed.

Boarding his private train back to his homeland, the regent spotted an attached extra sleeping coach. It was for Edmund Veesenmayer, the newly appointed minister and plenipotentiary in charge of directing the Hungarian government to carry out Reich policies. Just in case Horthy would call out the army for resistance once he reached Hungary, his train was stopped at the border and kept idle until eleven a.m. the next day, March 19. Meanwhile, starting just after midnight of that day, a large German force consisting of eleven divisions with tanks, paratroopers, and motorized guns crossed the border, reaching Budapest before dawn. By the time Horthy's train rumbled back to Budapest, the German army had occupied Hungary.

Edmund Veesenmayer, SS Brigadefuhrer (Brigadier General) and Reich Plenipo-
tentiary in charge of German occupation of Hungary, at "Trials of War
Criminals before the Nuremberg Military Tribunals" in 1948.

Adolf Eichmann, SS-Oberturm-
bannfuhrer (Lieutenant Colonel)
in charge of mass deportations to
ghettos and Auschwitz-Birkenau
of Hungarian Jews.

54

Courtesy of Yad Vashem

Laszlo Szalasi, leader of the anti-Semitic Arrow Cross political party in Hungary and prime minister during reign of terror at the end of 1944. He was sentenced to death as a war criminal.

The photos below and on the following pages show some of the first Jews from Hungary deported to Auschwitz-Birkenau relate the process of selection for genocide. They are from the Auschwitz Album, a collection of photographs held at Yad Vashem, taken by two SS guards in late May, 1944. After debarking the train, deportees are told to form two lines, women and children on one and men on the other. SS doctors at the head of each line select which are for labor or for annihilation—in the gas chambers. The women with children and old men facing imminent death are either ordered to walk for "showers" toward large brick buildings, which are actually the gas chambers/crematoriums, or wait in nearby woods for their time to take a "shower." Meanwhile, able-bodied men and women without children are allowed to survive as laborers under inhumane conditions.

Photos Courtesy of Auschwitz-Birkenau State Museum and Yad Vashem

CHAPTER SIX

"OPERATION HUNGARY"

Eichmann arrived in Budapest on March 19, the day of the invasion. His entourage included a dozen SS officers and a large coterie of secretaries, cooks, and chauffeurs. Eichmann was eager to get started coordinating the mass deportations, but he had to wait to align his job with the new quisling government that would answer to Veesenmayer. Horthy, meanwhile, tried to exert what little influence he still had with the Germans. After objecting to Veesenmayer's first choice for prime minister, he suggested as a compromise Domë Sztójay, Hungary's longtime ambassador to Germany and a well-known anti-Semite. Horthy had worked closely with Sztójay since 1935, and he wanted an ally in the new government. Andor Jaross, another notorious anti-Semite, joined Sztójay's cabinet as interior minister. László Endre, was appointed state secretary in the Minister of the Interior under Jaross; and László Baky became under state secretary in charge of "Jewish affairs." Known thereafter as the

"Deportation Trio," the three had command of the police, civil servants, and gendarmerie—all the resources Eichmann needed to control the country's Jewish population.

The official who was arguably most vital to Eichmann's plans in Hungary was László Ferenczy, a subordinate to Endre and Baky. He had gained the attention of the Germans in 1942 and 1943, when he helped them track down Slovakian refugees who had snuck into Hungary. He became head of a regional investigative unit of the Hungarian army before taking charge of the army's notoriously brutal gendarmerie unit. Boyish looking with slicked hair parted down the middle of his head, the forty-six-year-old lieutenant colonel was appointed liaison officer to Eichmann's staff by Interior Minister Jaross. Ferenczy was the link the Reich needed to bring home the invasion force. The more than 20,000 gendarmerie troops under Ferenczy's command, plus local police, would provide Eichmann and his meager SS unit with the muscle they needed to round up and deport Hungary's Jews.

Now the next step was to set up a system that would make the Jewish leaders instrumental in carrying out the Nazi game plan. It started within hours of the German occupation when several high-ranking German officers showed up at the Sip Street headquarters of the Jewish congregation on the Pest side of Budapest demanding that all reformed and orthodox leaders assemble there the next morning at 9:30. Some of the leaders sought out government officials that evening for advice, but the most they received was from the police chief the next morning who told them to comply with whatever the Germans want. "This reply decided the policy of the Jewish Council for months to come and, for all intents and purposes, settled the fate of Hungarian Jewry," wrote the Secretary of the Jewish Council Erno Munkacsi.[1]

Fearing they would be sent to a local criminal internment camp from their 9:30 meeting, some of the rabbis arrived with their wives and baggage. The meeting started out ominously when machine gun–toting Gestapo officers in leather coats walked in ahead of a Nazi civilian wearing a black bowler hat. He proceeded to greet them with instructions to form, by noon the next day, a national Jewish council. All Hungarian Jews would owe allegiance to the council, which would receive its orders from the German Secret Service. It was Eichmann's idea, aimed at giving the air of legitimacy by letting the assembled Jews choose the council members from a diversity of Jewish community leaders, civilian and reformed, orthodox and Zionist rabbis, and even Jewish converts to Christianity. A total of twenty-five men formed the National Jewish Council in Budapest, which then established administrative departments over housing, travel, and other elements of Jewish life. The Gestapo tapped into every phone call coming into and out of the council headquarters and administrative buildings. Over coming weeks, the SS under Eichmann set up another 150 such councils in the provinces. Before unleashing a crackdown on Hungary's Jews, Eichmann tried to appeal to them with sympathetic lies and threats. On March 31, he introduced himself to leaders of the new Jewish Council he had established to work with him and help placate the nation's Jewish population. "You know who I am, don't you?" he said. "I'm the one they call the bloodhound."[2]

Having established his authority, he turned amiable and courteous. Eichmann said his main task was to increase factory production for the war, and he needed Hungarian labor to do it. "If the Jews behave properly, they will suffer no harm whatsoever," he said.[3] He promised he would protect the Jews and that they would get paid the same as non-Jews for working in factories, clearing forests, or making gloves at home. He said that violence had occurred in other occupied countries only when the Jews had risen up in opposition. The council acquiesced, in part, because it believed that a revolt by some Jews would end disastrously for all of them. It also hoped that Hungary would join the Allies and the Allies would win the war before the Nazis could act on their hatred of the Jews. As Samu Stern, the president of the Jewish community in Budapest, told his colleagues, "We're running a race against time."[4] That acquiescence, however well intentioned, consisted of remaining silent and robbed Jews in the countryside of any chance to resist or evade deportation. On March 31, at Eichmann's first meeting with a select group of the National Council's leaders, he followed up his comments on needing the Jews only for labor with explicit instructions for all Hungarian Jews to start wearing a yellow star on their outer clothing starting on April 5. He told the Council to contact a factory immediately for three million stars of exact shape, color, and size. He suggested that 70,000 meters of fabric would be needed. All Jews would have to pay three Hungarian pengos for each star, with either the council or rich Jews paying for those too poor to pay.

A few days after receiving Eichmann's order to the council requiring the wearing of stars, Allied bombers, for the first time, struck at Budapest, destroying military targets and some residential areas. Immediately, the Sztójay government ordered that Jewish families had to vacate their apartments to be taken over by Christian families whose homes had been bombed. On April 4, Eichmann reinforced the order, screaming red faced at council members, *"Ich werde mit solchen Schlitten fahren"* (I'll rake you over the coals, if the evictions do not happen in the next 24 hours)."[5] Council members tried to explain that it "was impossible to carry out his order. Stomping his feet, he reiterated his threats of retribution and said he would have the Jews and their baggage thrown out into the street himself if the Council was incapable of vacating the flats on its own."[6] Frightened and aware they could be held accountable and replaced, the council members agreed. They told staff to accompany police and other government workers in the evacuation (leaving furnishings intact) of 1,500 Jewish-occupied apartments. By six p.m. the next day, when Jewish stars were first worn all over the country, 1,500 keys were delivered by the council to the government while shocked Jewish families scrambled to ask relatives, friends, and the council for a roof over their heads. They were barred from taking money, gold, or valuables, and were allowed to bring only fourteen days of food and a small amount of clothing.

Hungarian and German officials were eager to get their hands on the wealth of Hungarian Jews, both to help fund the war and to cover the cost of rounding up and deporting as many as 700,000 people. In addition, "The German invasion came as a godsend for many who aspired to the positions and assets of their Jewish neighbors. It seemed as if the collaborationist government fulfilled all the wishes of anti-Semites at once through the full scale nationalization of Jewish property, including apartments and shops."[7]

The wealth of Hungary's Jews at the time was estimated to be between seven and nine billion gold pengos ($239 million at the time).[8] Hungary even forced them to pay their 1944 taxes in advance. Every municipality helped with the confiscation effort, to the point of keeping an inventory of every item, valuable or not, taken from each household. Eichmann showed particular interest in the holdings and bank accounts of wealthy Budapest Jews. From two wealthy families alone his troops commandeered paintings by El Greco, van Dyck, Rembrandt, Rubens, and Gauguin.[9] Ferenczy's gendarmerie soldiers and Eichmann's SS forces marched into villages across Hungary to confiscate from Jewish families valuables including cash, jewels, gold, art, and silverware. They rounded up local leaders, giving them the choice of execution or identifying Jewish neighbors who had money. The subsequent confiscations left Hungary's Jews without funds to escape by rail or offer bribes for better treatment. It was all part of a grand plan for eventual deportation sanctioned by Baky and Endre in Budapest. Ferenczy euphemistically named his headquarters in Budapest "International Warehouse and Transport Ltd." But among those in the know, it was the "Hungarian Jew-Liquidating Command."[10]

The next step was concentrating the Jews into ghettos, which were established near train stations for the trip to Auschwitz. After forcing the Jews into makeshift ghettos, which were often open-air brickyards with little or no sanitary facilities, gendarmes searched them for hidden valuables. Cock-plumed gendarmes brutally forced the turnover of jewelry and other goods. They used rubber truncheons, electric currents to sex organs of men and women, punches, and needles under finger and toenails. Wives screamed from torture; husbands took knees to the groin; children fell bloodied in front of their parents. This happened in ghetto after ghetto. When the Jewish Council in Budapest had heard enough it sent a petition for mercy describing the wretched conditions in the ghettos, first to the Ministry of the Interior and then to Eichmann. In Kassa, it said, there was not enough food for the 11,500 detained there. In the northeastern city of Nyíregyháza, nearly 11,000 people were held in twenty-three buildings, with less than one square meter of space for each person. In Máramarossziget, in the southeast, atrocities by police and gendarmes included the raping of women and the use of midwives to examine young girls for hidden jewels.[11]

Over those last weeks of April 1944, while the ghettos were filled across Hungary, Eichmann prepared phase two of his plan: the deportations to Auschwitz. It began in late April with the transport of several thousand prisoners from the Kistarcsa internment camp outside Budapest, perhaps the same train that Ceslav saw arrive a few days later. The two transports that arrived carried some 3,800 Hungarian Jews aged sixteen to fifty. Weak from the horrible conditions in the ghetto, and sick from the stifling heat in the boxcars, they were of little use to the Germans. Only 486 men and 616 women were deemed fit enough to be admitted to the camp. The remaining passengers—2,698 men and women were marched immediately to the gas chambers.[12] In Kecskemét, about forty miles southeast of

Budapest, the families of some of the men deported on one of the first trains were thrilled to receive postcards from them, saying they were well. Their friends spread the word in the ghetto not to worry. But when the families of the men discussed what else the postcards said, they discovered a striking similarity. All of them had written, "I have arrived. I am well and going to work." And all of them came from a mysterious place postmarked as "Waldsee."[13] In truth, Waldsee was a fictional place, dreamed up by the Nazis as part of a disinformation campaign to help perpetuate the lie that Jews were being deported only to work on farms and in armaments factories. Eichmann had wanted to ensure that rumors sparked by the initial deportations didn't cause revolts in the ghettos. So SS guards forced Auschwitz's newest inmates to provide names of family or friends still in Hungary and then dictated what was said on each postcard, after which they were marched to the gas chambers. A similar deception had been used at Auschwitz on 15,000 deportees from the combination ghetto/concentration camp at Theresienstadt, in Bohemia in 1943 and the beginning of August 1944. But each arrival of Theresienstadt deportees was quarantined for six months in a special section of Auschwitz that resembled the relative comfort of where they had come from. In order to spread the word to the Czech government in exile and others that Auschwitz was a safe place, the transported Jews from Theresienstadt were told that to keep their privileges they had to write letters and postcards to friends and relatives in the ghetto that all was well. The quarantine period was to show that the model Theresienstadt ghetto was duplicated when prisoners came to Birkenau. Men, women, and children lived together in a separate family camp. Letters and postcards were sent back to the ghetto, saying all was well. When the World Jewish Congress sent food parcels to the Theresienstadt camp, prisoners were told to reply with thank-you notes. The head of the German Red Cross visited the camp in February 1944 and reported he was pleased. The deception had worked. Hungary at the time was about 40 percent larger than it had been in the aftermath of World War 1.

The Hungarian army's gendarmerie leadership divided Hungary into six zones for deportations. The first zone set for mass transports was in the northeast, while the last zone to be cleared out would be Budapest. To start the deportations of Jewish men, women, and children to Auschwitz, the Germans needed both the approval and the assistance of the Hungarian authorities. Veesenmayer insisted that formal diplomacy be followed, even though he knew it would simply be a pretense for allowing Hungary to continue calling itself a sovereign nation. So Eichmann and Ferenczy, who was also eager to get mass deportations underway, came up with a step-by-step scheme. First there had to be a reason to vacate the ghettos. They agreed that Ferenczy would meet with State Secretaries Endre and Baky and agree that, because of food shortages and unsanitary conditions in the ghettos, the Jews would have to return to their homes or be moved elsewhere.[14] Eichmann and Veesen-mayer then met with Endre, Baky, Prime Minister Sztójay, and other government officials on May 4. They pretended to mull the dilemma. No, returning Jews to their homes wouldn't work; Christian neighbors had already moved into many of those homes. As for finding new quarters elsewhere in Hungary, most of the likely areas were already battling a typhus and cholera epidemic. The prearranged solution, proposed by Sztójay to Veesenmayer, was that the Germans would allow the families of the men selected for work in Poland's war factories to join them in the transports for "resettlement," or *Ausiedlung.* Veesenmayer and Eichmann nodded their approval. Linking the deportation of able-bodied Jews with their families set the Hungarian Holocaust in motion.[15]

Arranging for enough trains to start mass deportations became Eichmann's next goal. "Jews cannot be left behind owing to (a) shortage of wagons. They must be crammed in!" he announced.[16] He wanted each train to carry up to 4,000 persons, more than twice the number when the same trains and number of boxcars were used to transport troops to the eastern front. Routing enough trains to Auschwitz was the subject of conference calls with Berlin in early May. There would be four freight trains per day. When not used for military transports, such freight cars usually bore cattle and livestock. Eichmann had originally wanted five daily transports out of his own desire and also to comply with SS Chief Himmler's order to accelerate the "Hungarian Operation." But Auschwitz Commandant Rudolf Höss argued that even the expanded killing facilities could not handle that many people each day. So Eichmann had to settle for no more than four trains on most days. Thus, the stage was set for the mass deportations to begin in mid-May. The Hungarian gendarmerie marched them from the ghettos to the trains. Armed with submachine guns, the gendarmes used rifle butts and whips while barking orders to move faster. Despite such treatment, most of the Jews went peacefully, still holding out hope that resettlement would lead to the promise of housing and work. But if local Christians tried to interfere, the gendarmes screamed at them to get back or jammed rifle butts into their stomachs.

Conditions on the transport trains were unbearable. Each of the carriages was crammed with up to one hundred people, who stood pressed against each other in stifling heat from the hot spring weather. There was little water, and only a bucket for a toilet. Human excrement carpeted the floor. Amidst the sobbing of children, adults cried out for food and water. No one answered their pleas. Many of the elderly fell dying on the floors, and others went mad, as was the case in a transport from the southern Hungarian city of Baja. When the car doors slid open for the first time in three and a half days, there were fifty-five dead Jews, three of them women aged 104, 102, and 92. Some 200 of the deportees had gone mad during the trip.[17] The Jewish leaders of Budapest didn't spread the word for revolt because they had hatched a plan with Waffen-SS Colonel Kurt Becher, who was on good terms with SS boss Heinrich Himmler, to save one million Jews if the Allies would provide 10,000 trucks to the Germans for use on the eastern front against Soviet forces. The Jewish leaders pestered the Allies to at least consider the plan. The American War Refugee Board allowed negotiations to continue as the only chance for the survival of Hungary's Jews. But Britain refused to bargain on anything that might delay Germany's defeat. It held to its initial advice to the WRB to not even consider this "sheer case of blackmail."[18]

Throughout May and early June, Budapest Jews grew to resent the council's leadership. It initially stemmed from council agents in the field and the many of the hundreds of Jewish employees at headquarters acting aloof and treating other Jews rudely because council staffers felt protected when overseeing activities of the rest of the Jews. Then as rumors and reports filtered into Budapest from the provinces about the harsh ghettos and deportations, fear spread, along with some gallows humor. As one joke went, a Jew is awakened in the night by a banging on his door. "Who's there?" he asks. "The Gestapo," comes the answer. "Thank God," says the Jew. "I thought it was the Jewish Council."[19] The Eichmann-appointed Jewish Council of Budapest knew what was going on and was castigated in a heated meeting on June 10 for not staging a resistance. A group of disgruntled Budapest Jews, led by a young Zionist, Pest physician Imre Varga, called for the meeting at the council's executive meeting room on Sip Street. It was full and hushed in silence after Dr. Varga's impassioned, agitated questions to the council included: "Don't you understand that our fathers, mothers, brothers and sisters are being shoved into freight cars by the Gendarmerie at the point of bayonets into the unknown, into annihilation, smothered in human excrement? How can we stand for this any longer?... We must shout out to the whole world that they are murdering us! We must resist instead of slavishly obeying their orders!" No one spoke until, in a calm voice, Council President Samu Stern said that the council "is doing everything humanly possible.... Any resistance on the part of us Jews would only lead to futile bloodshed and would collapse almost instantly."[20] Stern then rushed out of the room, while Dr. Varga and his supporters argued without success that more had to be done. The next day, in despair over the lack of action, Dr. Varga committed suicide.[21]

When the trains from Hungary arrived at Auschwitz-Birkenau, SS officers and doctors first separated men from women and children. Then each of those lines went through another selection. Able-bodied men, women, and children more than twelve years of age would survive as laborers. The doctors shunted young children, pregnant women, the infirm, and the elderly (anyone above fifty years of age) directly to the "baths." But that line went through one last selection, that of the Dr. Josef Mengele, for subjects for his medical experiments. At the gas chambers the word "showers" was written in several languages. When the prisoners were brought into the chamber area for undressing, the SS officers told them to tie both shoes together and put all their clothing in a pile, which they would receive after their showers. If the deportees asked for water, they were told that they would have coffee later. When all sexes and ages were naked and ordered to crowd together in the room for their shower, the door was slammed shut. A few minutes would pass before a trap door in the ceiling opened and Zyklon B pellets fell, dissolving into a deadly gas when exposed to the body heat of the victims inside the sealed gas chamber. Instantly people's lungs stung hot, and one after another they tumbled down in agony and died. After the new arrivals were gassed, inmates of a special commando extracted teeth for gold and silver and searched orifices for hidden gems and rings. Women had their hair shorn prior to going into the gas chamber. Cremated ashes were crushed to fine powder on a concrete platform before being deposited into pits and buried. Another commando unit collected clothing left in the changing rooms, sending Hungarian-labeled shorts, shirts, men's and women's underwear, suits, shoes, dresses, and babies' swaddling clothes for reuse by the German Textile Administration for resettled ethnic German, German-owned or -managed businesses, and others.[22]

As "Operation Hungary" was at its height, in late May and June 1944, SS Master Sergeant Otto Moll, a known sadist, was director of crematoriums. He oversaw everything from the arrival of the deportees to the handling of the "shower" deception to the flow of death. Often when the arriving men, women, and children were either too few or too many for the crematoriums, Moll shot them himself at the burning pits. If children cried too loudly or adults resisted, Moll would personally throw them alive into the flames. He once told a woman to jump about and sing as he shot Jews and pushed their bodies into the pits. She did as commanded, apparently hoping this might save her life. When the last Jew tumbled in after being shot, Moll turned to her. Terrified, she stopped singing and stared at him. Raising his pistol he shot her in the head and kicked her body into the pit.[23]

CHAPTER SEVEN

THE ESCAPE

Early in the afternoon on Saturday, May 26, 1944, two prisoners met at a crudely built bunker at the bottom of a gravel pit in a multi-acre work area. The entire Auschwitz-Birkenau camp had a mile and a quarter radius, with the outer work area comprising more than half the space. "Any problems?" Ceslav Mordowicz asked Arnost Rosin, as both slipped into electrician coveralls that would camouflage them once they escaped. "Would I be here if there was?" he replied, an edge to his voice.

Arnost recognized Ceslav as the leader of the escape but still took pride in being just as careful with his preparations. The two men discussed how they would manage in such a tight space for the next three days. Inside the bunker, they had stored a loaf of bread and a can of water. Two Polish prisoners, who had worked with Ceslav the past two weeks building the hiding place, nervously scanned the landscape for guards. "Cut the chit chat and get in," one of the men said. "We still have to get you covered."

Ceslav and Arnost crawled into the hole, which was approximately seven-feet long, six-feet wide at the deep end, and two-and-a half feet high. Arnost, who was the taller of the two, took the longer inside position. At five-foot-eight, Ceslav had to bend his knees a bit to squeeze beside him. "My first mistake," Ceslav said. "I should have made sure it would be wide enough." Then the burial of the two began. First the Polish workers secured a wooden roof over the sloping entrance, supported by wooden timbers. Then they inserted a one-inch-thick lead air pipe through the roof, before covering it with rocks, dirt, and loose grass sprinkled with turpentine, to mask their scent from the SS dogs. Ceslav uncorked the air pipe, tasted fresh air, and gave two knocks on the roof for approval. Their tasks done, the two fellow prisoners walked quickly away in opposite directions, leaving Ceslav and Arnost inside the bunker in pitch-black darkness. The two lay side by side, with just enough room for each of them to reach up and draw air from the pipe.

"Nothing will happen for a few hours until they find us missing," Ceslav said. Guards had been checking the ID numbers of prisoners in the work area every two hours since Wetzler and Rosenberg had escaped more than a month earlier. Around four o'clock that afternoon, roughly three hours after the pair had taken their place in the bunker, the sirens began wailing. "That's for us," Ceslav said, as he tensed at the sound. The dirt did little to muffle it. He and Alfred had not been accounted for at the two p.m. check-in, and a preliminary search by guards of their assigned work areas came up empty. Now the search was on. Would the plan work? Had they forgotten something? Although Ceslav had been over his checklist innumerable times, he couldn't help but review it again. This time, like all the others, he stopped at each detail and imagined unforeseen things happening. He tried to engage Arnost in his game of "What if," but Arnost would have no part of it. "Stop it, will you? We are here now and there is nothing to do but lie and wait."

Yet Arnost sensed something drastic had gone wrong. At first, he thought it was his own nervousness, which would pass. But the more he tried to calm himself down, the harder it was for him to breathe. He reached for the pipe and sucked for air. No! It can't be, he thought. There were only traces of air, not life-sustaining gulps. "It's not coming. The air's not coming through the hole the way it should," he whispered urgently.

"The pipe was clear when I tested it," Ceslav said. He took Arnost's place at the pipe and was no more successful. Somewhere in its three-foot length there was an obstruction. Ceslav tore a splinter from the beam beside his head and stuck it as far into the pipe as he could. It dislodged nothing. They speculated that their helpers may have panicked and purposely blocked the air passage after Ceslav's signal. Maybe they wanted Ceslav and Arnost to suffocate so they could not give up the Poles' names if they were caught and tortured.

Sweating, Ceslav lay back down and reached across Arnost for the can of water. It was lighter than it should be, considering it was supposed to last three days. Would Arnost have taken so much in the first few hours? No, Ceslav remembered each of them had only had a sip since entering the hole. He reached down to touch the dirt and, as he feared, found it soaked. In their rush to get air from the pipe, one of them had apparently knocked the can over, spilling most of the contents. All of a sudden, their plan was unraveling.

Not long after the alarms sounded, the search for the missing prisoners began. Guards and packs of dogs prowled every inch of the one and a half mile diameter work area. "Our worry now is how well camouflaged we are from the top," Ceslav noted. Hearing the barking, Arnost replied, "We'll soon find out." They could hear an SS guard shouting. "They must be caught! Must be caught!" The minutes seemed like hours. Over and over voices receded, came back stronger, and then faded away again.

Not knowing if it was day or night, Ceslav and Arnost lay in darkness, sweating from the heat, growing weaker from lack of air, and wishing they could smoke one of their homemade cigarettes. Ceslav began digging his way for air, careful not to disturb the camouflaged roof. The best he could do was create a hole about the width of two fingers beside the roof. It helped a bit but was no substitute for the air pipe, had it been working. "We're going to die in here," Ceslav said, "unless we leave before the three-day search is called off." But both of them had heard enough shots in the night during previous attempted escapes to know that they would be easy targets if they crawled out too early. "We'll see how it goes for another day," Ceslav said.

The sound of barking dogs awoke them the following morning. Suddenly, as if the dogs knew exactly where they were hiding, the barking grew louder. Within seconds, the two startled men heard scratching on the surface of their bunker. In their minds they saw the scene above—the packs of dogs eagerly clawing at the earth as if in search of a bone, the guards ready to rip off the wooden roof and point rifle barrels at their upturned faces. Why isn't the scent of the turpentine driving the dogs away? Ceslav wondered. He dared not say anything to Arnost for fear of being heard. Yet he wanted to scream as the furious scratching over his head got louder and louder.

The next moment there was no sound at all. Had the dogs found something? Were the guards getting ready to rip the roof off? Minutes passed. "They're gone," whispered Arnost. The turpentine had apparently worked after all. "Let's drink to our small victory," Ceslav said. Even though they had only a few drops of water left, Arnost nodded. He needed to boost his spirits as much as he needed the precious liquid. Throughout the rest of the day they heard guards and dogs searching the area, but never as close again. Now, their greatest fear was suffocation, which was slowly killing both of them. Without enough air, their minds grew dizzy and their bodies began to swell. Ceslav touched his forehead. It was like putting his finger into a stick of butter. He knew Arnost was undergoing the same bizarre sensations. Yet they had to endure. With the guards still combing the grounds, leaving the bunker now would mean certain capture.

"We have to do something," Arnost said in a weak whisper. Each of them had stretched as close as they could to the air gap in the dirt, but the effort took more out of them than it was worth. When Ceslav desperately tried to expand the hole, sand poured in before his fingers reached the outer edge. Through the opening they could see it was still daylight. Weak and exhausted, they assumed the end was near. "At least we tried" was all Arnost could say after Ceslav thanked him for having enough faith to go this far. A few hours later, Ceslav realized he could no longer see light from the air hole. He listened for sounds of the dogs and guards. Nothing. "Now! We have to try now," he told Arnost, not knowing if he was dead or alive. Arnost stirred as Ceslav turned feebly on his side to claw sand away to widen the hole. But with his hands so swollen, he didn't have the strength. "Arnost, you try. I'm no good."

Crawling over him, Arnost pushed up against the roof, hoping the dirt and rocks would give way. Nothing happened, other than a shower of sand. Frantically, he clawed at the hole in the sand. It tumbled in more heavily and yet still there was no surge of air. With their faces only inches apart, they could feel each other's breath and the fear of death. Suddenly, Ceslav's fist was outside their tomb. With one desperate punch he had burst through. "Arnost, dig next to my hand! It's opening." Soon, both of their hands were on the outside of the bunker and air was flowing freely around them. But they lacked the strength to push the roof away, no matter how hard they tried. Their hands and feet were numb. Ceslav imagined them still trapped inside the bunker in the morning, as the search team discovered the hole that had brought them needed air but not a way out.

As they regained some of their strength, Ceslav and Arnost gingerly pulled sand away from one hole and started another. This went on for several hours. Neither of the men said much, knowing they were racing against the clock. When they had cleared two holes several inches wide on each side of the roof, they turned their full attention to pushing the roof open. Ceslav squirmed around to position himself on his back with his knees bent and feet set beside Arnost's hands. "When I say go, go,"

Ceslav told Arnost. The roof fell away as rocks, then dirt poured into the hole. One final shove moved the door far enough aside for each of them to crawl out. Ceslav went first, reaching in to pull Arnost up. Kneeling beside the open bunker, neither of them had the strength to stand.

It was still dark outside. Despite their weakened state, they had to move fast, as they only had a few hours before daybreak. Forgetting the extra loaf of bread they had stored, they crawled quickly to the top of the quarry to get their bearings. The manned guard posts surrounding the work area were several hundred yards away. Once they reached them, they would need to sneak between two of the three-legged, two-story-high posts stationed eighty-seven yards apart. The guards at the posts wouldn't be withdrawn until the three-day search for the men had ended. That wouldn't happen for another twenty-four hours. Ceslav and Arnost were risking sure death by leaving their bunker early.

No sooner had they stood up than they saw a motorcycle headlight approaching from about one hundred yards away. "Could they be coming for us?" Arnost asked Ceslav. "No. It must just be a patrol. Lie down." The motorcycle veered off, shining light on a guard post about a quarter mile away. The dog pound was in that same area, Ceslav noted as he turned to face the opposite direction. After spending nearly two days in the pitch-black bunker, the men had trouble seeing more than a few feet in front of them. Everything appeared to be in darkness. So Arnost was surprised when Ceslav grabbed his arm and began leading him with assurance. "How do you know where you are going?" Arnost asked. For the past several weeks during the daytime, Ceslav had practiced walking from the bunker toward the guard posts with his eyes closed. Now he slowly led them step by step.

Their only landmark for direction was the flames coming from the crematorium. At one point, after they had walked about 150 yards, they stopped hand in hand and looked at the flames—aware of how far they had come and how far they still had to go to earn their freedom. As they walked farther, Ceslav pointed to the work shed that his commando used. When they reached it, they found a local worker from the town of Auschwitz asleep on a cot. Pretending to be drunken SS soldiers, Ceslav and Arnost yanked open the door and demanded something to drink. The startled worker handed the men a can of cold coffee, which they quickly drank before continuing on.

As usual, there were no lights at the guard posts. That was a small comfort, however. Ceslav and Arnost knew their powerful searchlights would be switched on at the sound of the slightest unfamiliar noise. Many prisoners trying to escape had gotten this far before being spotted by a guard at one of the posts and getting killed by machine gun fire. "We have to start crawling now," Ceslav said. Their jaws tightened, and fear gripped their bodies. They slowly moved forward, stopping every ten yards like dogs on point. They knew the guards were ahead of them, but they still could not make out the towers in the darkness. Ceslav's aim was to crawl at an equal distance between the guard posts. That meant leaving about forty-three yards of space on each side, enough, he hoped, to keep the guards from hearing scuffling sounds as the prisoners inched forward. Helping to muffle their movements were the arrivals of Hungarian transports, the whistling of locomotives, the shouting of guards, and the barking of dogs. Hearts pumping wildly, they feared that any moment the lights would switch on and shots would ring out. Ceslav squeezed his eyes shut and kept crawling. Eventually he could see the outlines of guard posts along the edge of the work area. He put his hand on Arnost's shoulder, indicating he should stop. Sooner or later, one of the guards would cough, sneeze, or shuffle his feet on the wooden platform. That would help determine the route they would take as they crawled between the two posts.

"Aargh." The sound of a guard clearing his throat came from about fifty yards in front of them to their right. Ceslav and Arnost began crawling diagonally toward the left, faster than before. They knew they would be in so-called "no-man's-land" when they started downhill. That would be the gulch dug just before the guard post perimeter. But as they continued crawling, there was no sign of a gulch. Were they going in circles? After an hour, Ceslav stopped and looked up to see if the watchtowers were still in front of them. They weren't. Apparently the two had crawled down and up the gulch and passed between the guard towers without knowing it. Now they were well behind the towers on the outside of the camp. They could tell because the flames of Auschwitz's crematoriums were now behind the guard posts.

Ceslav turned toward Arnost and grabbed his hand. "Stand up, we have to run." They took off, heading through a lightly wooded area toward the Sola River, which was about two miles away and served as the border for the town of Auschwitz. Crossing that river would be another step toward freedom.

But the prisoners didn't know how much time they had until dawn. Stumbling and running to the point of exhaustion and then walking to catch their breath, they finally came to the edge of the river. Still swollen from spring rains, it was wide and deep—a problem for Ceslav, as he couldn't swim.

Now it was Arnost's turn to take charge. He told Ceslav to take his shoes and clothes off and to wrap them in a bundle. Arnost did the same and related his plan. While holding his clothing bundle aloft in one hand he would swim to the other side of the river, and then he would come back and pull Ceslav across in the same manner. The plan worked fine at first. After forging the river and depositing his shoes and clothing on the shore, he swam back, picked up a stick and told Ceslav to hold on. Ceslav's shoes slipped out of his bundle during the crossing. "Now we each have one shoe," Arnost said, handing one of his shoes to the apologetic Ceslav after they reached the shore. To protect the other foot, each of them made a bandage with wadded underpants layered with strips torn from their shirts tied tight. They then headed east toward Krakow, about thirty-two miles away.

Ceslav had heard that in Krakow there was an underground resistance movement that would take them in. If they were lucky and smart enough to avoid capture, the trip would take a week at most. They would travel at night, sticking close to the road, and spend their days in the woods. The escapees suddenly came upon an obstacle Ceslav had not expected. He knew there would be railroad tracks to cross, but he had not known that they were bordered by a high, barbed wire fence. "You first," Ceslav said to Arnost. "You're taller and have a better chance of making it." Arnost clambered over the top and dropped to the other side. But as Ceslav reached the top and was about to drop down, the palm of his hand caught a sharp edge. "Shit!" he said, knowing the last thing he needed was an infected hand. Blood ran off his fingertips as he and Arnost scurried away into the woods. Once there, Ceslav stopped and wrapped the wound with another piece of cloth from his shirt.

"Which way?" Arnost asked. Taking the lead, Ceslav made surprisingly good progress in the darkness. Luckily the underbrush had not yet thickened and most of the trees were tall enough so the two men could pass beneath their branches. They alternately ran and walked. As they headed deeper and deeper into the woods, they covered at least ten miles before they fell to the ground exhausted at dawn. Meanwhile, the Auschwitz search party came upon the abandoned bunker early that morning. On May 28, at 1800 hours, the SS sent a telegram alerting "ALL EASTERN GESTAPO CENTERS" to the "Fleeing of prisoners" Mordowicz and Rosin.[1] Alerting Berlin about the prisoners' escape was not a formality. As Jews with intimate knowledge of the Auschwitz-Birkenau death camp, the two were as dangerous to the Nazis as traitorous spies. They had to be found and brought back.

Ceslav and Arnost awoke just as the sun was setting. It was time to resume their flight near the road through the forest. They had not gotten far when they had to cross a wooden bridge over a ravine. Halfway across they saw SS troops coming toward them. Ceslav and Arnost, still in their coveralls, quickly put on their electrician hats and sat down, dangling their feet over the edge of the bridge and pointing to the wires running above that brought electricity to the nearby village of Chelmek. Pretending to be weighing a problem, Ceslav and Rosin kept talking and pointing to the wires as the SS troops marched by without incident. The twosome then went to the other side of the bridge, where they found a grove of turnips. Dirty but tasty, the turnips were Ceslav and Arnost's first breakfast before resuming their journey. After another few hours of walking in the woods, hunger gripped their bodies. On the verge of grabbing clumps of grass to eat, they spotted a small house with a fence, hoping that they could at least get a piece of bread and some water to drink. Suddenly a lady of fifty to fifty-five years of age came out of the house and started hanging laundry. Ceslav approached her gingerly, telling her in Polish she needn't be afraid; they only wanted a piece of stale bread. She said, " I will give you a piece of bread and even some milk." Ceslav and Arnost took her offering, with Ceslav murmuring, "It's like a piece of life itself. Thank you." She replied, "Boys, be careful. I ask you, please, run away from here. Last night in this forest there was a German raid, even with tanks. I don't know what they were looking for. But they searched the whole place."

Several miles more through a forest they reached the Vistula River, snaking south to north through Poland. There, about nine miles from Krakow, Ceslav offered to make a trade with a youth running a small boat service. Ceslav's side of the swap was the watch that came with his workman's clothes. He offered it to the boy in exchange for passage across the lake and the lad's boots. Over the next week the two men kept to a routine of sleeping during the daytime and walking and running at night. During that time, trainloads of unsuspecting Hungarian Jews were deposited at death's door in Auschwitz. From May 17, when Ceslav and Arnost hid in their bunker, through May 31, forty kilograms of gold were taken from the teeth of Hungarian Jewish corpses.

One morning, just as dawn was breaking and they were getting ready to bed down for the day, they came across another small house where a woman was beginning a chore. Ceslav once again politely asked for a price of bread. The woman said, "Why, yes, I will give it to you. I will even give you some soup. But cut up this wood for me, which needs chopping." She gave each of them an ax and when they were finished, rewarded them with eggs, soup, bread, and white coffee. The escapees were fortunate those were the two women they met and that they were Polish. For forty square kilometers around Auschwitz, the SS had forced most Polish families to turn their homes over to loyal Germans. When a prisoner escaped, SS men would scour the area, first grilling the remaining Polish families for what they knew and had seen. The women Ceslav and Arnost met apparently kept their secret. Not everyone was so kind; others who were asked for help eyed them with distrust. Barely finding the strength to keep walking, they fell into despair and feared they would be caught and brought back to Auschwitz. Instead of feeling free, the same lurking danger that had gripped them in the camp for years was with them in the open.

Their plan of reaching Warsaw, where they had expected to fall in with friendly resistance fighters, had already given them a setback. From one of the friendly Polish women, they learned that German forces were thick in the woods and towns to the north, searching for men and boys to dig trenches in the eastern front. "We need to go south to Slovakia, not north to Warsaw," Arnost told Ceslav. Ceslav agreed because there were still some Jews there even though many had been deported and Slovakia was in the German camp. The escapees had already traveled more than twenty-five miles from Auschwitz, but it was still about forty-five miles and over the Tatra Mountains to the Slovakian border. They came upon a railway station, where they learned a train would be coming through within the next hour on its way toward Nowy Targ, a small town not far from the border. "We have no money," Ceslav told a railway clerk. Taking pity, the clerk confided that the roof of the train offered "a wonderful view" of the countryside. So they hid in a toilet closet until just before they heard the train whistle and then climbed to the roof. Before reaching Nowy Targ, where troops would be meeting trains to inspect documents, Ceslav and Arnost jumped from the train as it slowed around a corner. They were still eight miles from the border, so they slept in the woods before resuming their hike through meadows and over high hills.

Finally, at the top of a hill, they saw a river that they assumed had to lead to Czarny Dunajec, a small village that was on the Slovakia border. They knew the landscapes of Poland and Slovakia well from their school days; Ceslav was Polish and Arnost was a Slovak. The swirling water of the river was not very deep, so they crossed by foot. On the other side, Ceslav and Arnost walked into a grove of trees where Ceslav picked up a match box that read *Slovenske zápalki*, which translated was "Slovak matches." Arnost grabbed the match box away from Ceslav and would have jumped for joy if he weren't so weak.

"We are in Slovakia. I am home," he exclaimed. They climbed another hill. Upon reaching the top, Arnost said, "Look down below, a village store. I must have a drink of beer. I must light up a cigarette. I am home." Ceslav replied sternly, "Arnost, no! Remember Slovakia is also run by the Germans." He also reminded Arnost that he didn't have any money. But Arnost paid no mind, saying abruptly, "They'll give it to me. I'm going. If you don't like it, you go your own way."

Ceslav took Arnost's remark personally, given all they had been through together. Nonetheless, he waited outside the store, keeping watch for German soldiers. When Arnost stepped back outside, he asked if the beer was good. "God damn him. He did not want to give it to me without money." Just then, a farmer in a horse and wagon came by. Arnost asked in Slovakian if he would give them a ride. "You have not heard what they were saying on the radio?" he asked the men. It was June 6, 1944, the day of the Allied invasion at Normandy, France. "Boys, today I invite you for a beer. We are going to the tavern." Ceslav wagged his finger at Arnost. But Arnost persisted, and so Ceslav, against his better judgment, entered the tavern with him. It was only midafternoon, but the room was full. Men jumped to their feet, welcoming them. They had heard about the invasion on the radio. More than one of the locals said, "This round is on me; let's drink." Before long, as the party was roaring, two Slovak gendarmes—who supported the Reich and were searching for partisan revolutionaries—showed up and walked straight toward Arnost and Ceslav, asking them for their papers. The owner of the store where Arnost had tried to buy a beer had denounced him as suspicious to the gendarmes.

Ceslav turned to Arnost, saying, "Well, you better start talking. I don't know Slovak." Arnost was no help. "In the name of the law you are under arrest and must come with us to the command post," said one of the gendarmes. As he led the two men out of the tavern, he added, "If you try to run away, we shoot to kill." Ceslav fumed. "See what you've done," he told Arnost. "This was the beginning of our freedom." At the gendarme command post, Arnost maintained he had been born in the town of Snina, in eastern Slovakia. It did him no good. After asking a few questions, the commandant concluded they must be Jewish escapees from a German concentration camp. He said he would send them back to the Polish border into German hands. Ceslav resisted, saying he would not go alive. So the commandant ordered the two to be taken to the regional court at Spišská Stará Ves, where a hearing would determine what to do with them. In the court's corridor, Arnost spotted a childhood friend and asked their guard to call him over. "Arnost, what are you doing here?" the man asked, astonished. "They deported you in '42." Arnost told him the situation and asked for his help. "Listen," his friend said, "there is still a small Jewish community here. I will let them know that you're here."

Two hours later, a short man appeared outside the bars of their cell. "I am Mangel," he said in Slovakian. "Where did you come here from?" Arnost told him about Auschwitz, pleading for him to do something that would keep the Germans from sending them back. Alex Mangel was with the Zionist Jewish community of Slovakia, based in Bratislava, which had raised money from wealthy Jews in late 1942 to bribe German officials in exchange for a halt to the deportations. Mangel told Ceslav and Arnost he would be back that evening. When he returned, he gave Ceslav and Arnost each a one-dollar banknote, and told them to make sure it was showing from their breast pockets when they went to their hearing the following morning. It would appear as if they had been at the border with foreign currency.

The plan worked. The next day, the two men were charged with currency smuggling, sentenced to prison and fined. The town's Jewish leaders paid the fine. As the jailer opened the cell door, Arnost slapped Ceslav on the back, and both sighed with relief. They were free to go.

*Ceslav Mordowicz,
first official photo
after WWII, 1947*

Arnost Rosin

Courtesy of the Simon Wiesenthal Center Archives, Los Angeles, California, and Getty Images NA

*Walter Rosenberg (Rudolf Vrba)
(above) and Alfred Wetzler (left)
escaped from Auschwitz-Birkenau
on April 7, 1944*

Jaromír Kopecký, a Czech Republic in Exile official based in Switzerland who was the conduit to diplomats of the Western Allies and the Vatican for all the reports in the Auschwitz Protocols.

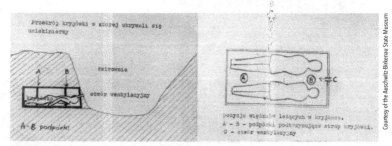

Drawing by Ceslav Mordowicz of the bunker in the gravel pit at Auschwitz-Birkenau where they hid until their escape.

CHAPTER EIGHT

"ALL IS LOST"

Leaving the prison, Mangel drove the two men to a nursing home in Liptovský Mikuláš, a small town in northern Slovakia, where the two escapees could recuperate. On the way, Ceslav kept telling Mangel, "You must stop the transports." Ceslav had already informed him about the arrival of the Hungarian Jews at Auschwitz. "Get your strength back and then we'll talk," said Mangel. The next day, Mangel took Ceslav and Arnost to visit leading Jewish businessmen in the area. Although the Slovak authorities had deported roughly 60,000 Jews into German custody in 1942, the Jewish leadership had no reliable information on what happened to those deported. Many prominent Slovakian Jewish families remained untouched, including the owners of Liptovský Mikuláš's many leather factories. One in particular, a wealthy aristocrat named Rudolf Haas, refused to believe what the two escapees were telling him.

"Both of you are insane," said Haas. "They need laborers for their war. That is all." Incensed, Ceslav put down his cup of coffee and leaned forward in his chair. In a slow, low voice he began speaking in Yiddish to emphasize their common bond. "When you learn that what we have said is true, remember this day and that we came to warn you of the danger you and all Jews are facing." Ceslav and Arnost rose together. Both turned and left without shaking Haas's hand.

Clearly, the Auschwitz escape two months earlier by Walter Rosenberg (Rudolf Vrba) and Alfred "Fredo" Wetzler and the details they told about the murders of European Jews by poisoned gas had not raised widespread alarm. The world was still ignorant of the Holocaust, even though verifiable reports of Nazi atrocities against the Jews had been known to the Allies for years. Vrba and Wetzler had hidden for three days and nights inside a woodpile bunker, on the outer perimeter of a new work area at Auschwitz. When the nighttime guards exited the watchtowers, they fled the camp and walked eighty miles over eleven days before a farmer saw them hobbling toward the Slovakian border. He took them to a local Jewish doctor, who bandaged Vrba's ravaged feet, and arranged for a meeting with officials from the Jewish community leadership in Slovakia.

Oskar Krasnansky, a chemical engineer; Dr. Oskar Neumann, a German-speaking lawyer; and leaders of the Jewish Central Council (JCC) of Bratislava interviewed them together and in different rooms over three days. Vrba and Wetzler had a deep knowledge of the inner workings of the camp. Vrba had worked in a "Clearing Commando" that dragged out dead bodies from each train of deportees. Then he and Wetzler, as clerks of their barracks, had daily contact with other clerks as well as with the prisoners assigned to help process new arrivals. One part of the Vrba/Wetzler account seemed unbelievable: a tabulation of 1,765,000 Jews killed at Auschwitz in the two years before their escape. Among their ways of keeping a running tally of Jews arriving was noting how many trucks full of Jews passed their barracks on the way to the crematoriums from the rail depot two miles away. Krasnansky had brought with him JCC statistics on the number of Jews taken from Slovakia (60,000) and the dates of deportations. When he asked about Slovakia, the two escapees cited dates and numbers that coincided exactly with his information.

Convinced that their accounts of Auschwitz were true, Krasnansky took copious notes on descriptions of the barracks, kitchens, and hospital as well as details on processing, gassing, and tattooing of incoming deportees. Vrba and Wetzler each wrote a portion of their Auschwitz Protocols. From their interviews, Krasnansky also produced architectural drawings of a combined gas chamber and crematoria. There were four at the time of their escape, with the reception halls of the larger ones holding up to 2,000 imminent victims. The floor below, where prisoners were told to take off their clothes in preparation for a shower, could accommodate the same number of people. Krasnansky returned to Bratislava, where he and other council members sent typewritten copies of his report to the Orthodox Jewish Agency in Istanbul, Jewish leaders in Switzerland, the Czech diplomat Jaromir Kopecky in Switzerland, the Papal Nuncio Giuseppe Burzio in Bratislava, and the Orthodox Jewish leader Rudolf Kasztner in Budapest.[1]

Some of the Vrba/Wetzler report were abbreviated, twenty-page versions; others were as long as sixty pages. By the end of May, Rabbi Dov Weissmandel, who sent some of the reports, was stunned at the lack of reaction, the silence, and seeming disregard by Hungary's Jewish leaders and governments of the free world when confronted with mass murders. Some readers of the news found it too incredible to believe and reminded them of the exaggerated atrocities both sides charged against the other in the First World War. In a few instances, the lack of response was understandable. The report sent to the leaders of the Jewish Agency in Istanbul never arrived because the courier it had been entrusted to was a German spy.[2] Another copy, written in Yiddish, couldn't be read by some Jewish leaders in Geneva. But the Jewish leaders of Hungary, who would have been expected to rally to the cause, immediately read the report and remained silent. They had just begun negotiations with Eichmann on a Nazi offer to exchange one million Jewish lives for 10,000 trucks.

Eichmann told the Jewish leaders of Budapest in early April, "If my generous offer is accepted," he would save "'all' of the one million Hungarian Jews." If not, they will all be gassed."[3] It was a bluff by Himmler and Eichmann to buy time while they deported Hungarian Jews by the tens of thousands each week. To the Hungarian Jewish leaders, the potential deal was seen as more likely to help save Hungarian Jews than stirring up a deadly revolt.

Tragically, while the Vrba/Wetzler report was going unheeded, the mass annihilation of Hungarian Jews at Auschwitz-Birkenau continued at a record pace. Needed was more proof. It came with the testimony of Ceslav and Arnost in early June. After Mangel secured their release from prison, he took them to the home of another local Jewish leader for lunch. There, in a screened sun porch, they were greeted by an astonishing sight: the two men who had escaped Auschwitz just before them. Ceslav had not known Walter Rosenberg (who had not yet taken the name of Rudolf Vrba). But when he saw his friend Alfred Wetzler he embraced him, choking back tears of joy.

Before long, the four men were swapping stories of their escapes. Now, Ceslav informed Vrba and Wetzler that while they were telling the world about what was happening at Auschwitz, deportees from Hungary began appearing at the camp. "You wouldn't believe how fast they are killing the Hungarian Jews." Just then Krasnansky and several other Slovakian Council leaders arrived at the house to interview Ceslav and Arnost. If the new escapees (Ceslav and Arnost) independently reported that they also were witness to the mass gassings at Auschwitz of deported Jews, the council could renew its pleas for help with the corroborative testimony. "Please don't be offended. But we need to compare what each of you has to say about Auschwitz," said Krasnansky, who conducted the new interview.

Ceslav and Arnost went to another room while Rosenberg (Vrba) and Wetzler stayed on the porch. Krasnansky and the other Council leaders went back and forth between the two groups of men, cross examining them about "normal camp life," as well as the mass killings. What Ceslav and Arnost told them matched with Vrba's and Wetzler's accounts, including the time, in March 1944, when SS officials and Nazi Party members visited Auschwitz to inspect the first gassings at a new crematorium. The officials, including Reichsführer-SS Heinrich Himmler, took turns watching the killings through a peephole in the door and later praised the efficiency of the new hall.

After an initial round of interviews, Vrba and Wetzler went back to the safe house the local Jewish group had set up for them in a nearby town while Krasnansky stayed with Ceslav and Arnost. He asked them about what they had witnessed at Auschwitz in the weeks following the escape of the other two. Ceslav and Arnost recounted how, in mid-May, the "exterminating capacity" of the camp became "almost unlimited" as the Hungarian Jews began arriving at the rate of 6,000 to 12,000 per day. The vast majority of the deportees were sent to the gas chambers immediately. Since the establishment of Birkenau in 1942, never had so many Jews been gassed at such a staggering rate their report said, adding that "the 'Clearing Commando' was stepped up from 150 to 700 men." Their job was to take bodies from the gas chamber, inspect them for hidden gems, extract gold teeth, and cut the women's hair before bringing them to the ovens for burning. Three crematoria worked day and night (the fourth was being repaired at the time), and since the capacity of the crematoria was not large enough for all the bodies, huge burning pits thirty meters long and fifteen meters wide had to be dug to dispose of all the bodies. Even the gas chambers could not accommodate all the chosen victims right away. Old men, women, and children were marched to a wooded area, where they waited without a clue as to what was imminent.

His interviews with Ceslav and Arnost done, Krasnansky returned to Bratislava to discuss with the full Jewish Council what to do with the new information. Adding the new testimony, Krasnansky believed, would buttress the council's case that the Vrba/Wetzler report deserved immediate attention and action. The council agreed. Whether Krasnansky interviewed Mordowicz and Rosin immediately after the Jewish council paid their fine, as historian Martin Gilbert and others maintain, or after an eight day stay in prison is not clear. The records of the jail in Spišská Stará Ves are no longer available. Either way, between June 9 and June 17, "I put the two reports together and prepared to send them off again," Krasnansky said.[4] The Swiss communique he sent again reached Jaromir Kopecky in Geneva, who was ambassador for the Czech government in exile. Kopecky had already served as the key link to reaching the diplomatic community of Western diplomats, not only for the report of Ceslav and Arnost and Vrba/Wetzler, but also that of Jerzy Tabeau, also known as the "Polish Major," in November 1943. (All those reports eventually became the Auschwitz Protocols.) Tabeau's report was more about the brutalities and medical experiments of prisoners than gas chamber deaths, which may be one reason why his reference to gassings was not as shocking as the other two reports.

Kopecky's third try was more successful. He relayed both the Mordowicz/Rosin and Vrba/Wetzler reports to Geneva, where diplomats in turn alerted the Allies both of the truth of Auschwitz and of the annihilation of the so-called model labor camp there for Jews of Theresienstadt, Czechoslovakia. The reports that led the West to recognize the Holocaust for the first time said that more than 1.5 million European Jews had been massacred in Auschwitz gas chambers and urged fast action to save a second group of Theresienstadt Jews from a gassing scheduled for the twentieth of June.

Not long after Ceslav and Arnost gave their testimony, they met again with Vrba and Wetzler. This time they gathered at a well-furnished apartment on a hill in Bratislava, which overlooked the sprawling city on the Danube River and its centuries-old Jewish quarter. To avoid detection by German troops, Ceslav and Arnost arrived by car late at night. Safely hidden away in the apartment on the hill, and with the horrors of Auschwitz behind them, the four did what any young men would do: they had a good time. Arnost drank his favorite beer, and for the first time in years, there was laughter amidst the tears. "Great, great joy, great joy," Ceslav recalled later. He was able to put aside, at least for those moments, the anguish over the loss of his wife and his entire family. Though still weak, he had fiber to his voice and a lively spirit that impressed his friend Alfred. "You've got more get-up-and-go than me," said Alfred, noting that it had taken him at least a month to recover following his own escape.

Ceslav and Arnost were eager to hear how Vrba and Wetzler got out of Auschwitz alive. Their ordeal was equally chilling and fraught with danger.[5] It began with them donning well-made Dutch suits, overcoats, and heavy boots before taking positions in an empty space amidst a pile of wooden boards in the work area known as "Mexico." Almost immediately after discovering the two prisoners were missing from the evening roll call, dozens of guards and their dogs were combing every inch of the multi-acre work area, intent on upending any possible hiding spot. Boots and voices of soldiers and the panting of dogs could be heard as they stumbled across the planks of the woodpile. The tobacco soaked with gasoline drove the dogs away, and Vrba put away the knife he had drawn if they had been discovered. Two days later, two of the guards surmised the dogs may have been put off the scent, and they began removing the wood above Vrba and Wetzler. Cowering and ready to strike out with their knives, the escapees breathed a sigh of relief when the guards were called away.

The next night, the patrols were withdrawn on the assumption that there had been a successful escape. Counting on that, the two pushed away the rest of the wood covering. They scrambled past the empty guard towers into the forest, hoping their gentlemanly clothes would keep suspicion at bay from an outside rife with German troops and frightened, usually complicit, German and Polish families. Running across open land just outside the Auschwitz-Birkenau camp, Vrba and Wetzler bedded down in a clump of bushes in the first wooded area they came across. Unfortunately, they were in a public park frequented by SS troops and their families. They found that out as they awoke in daylight and saw an armed, uniformed soldier with a blond-haired wife on his arm and two small children bounding ahead toward the hideout bushes. Spotting Vrba and Wetzler on the ground in the bushes, the little girl yelled, "Pappa...Pappa...Come here....There are men in the bushes...funny men." The father came over, looked down at the two men, put his arm around his children, and whisked them away with his wife. Vrba and Wetzler didn't mind that the misassumptions about their moral behavior most likely saved their lives.

Five days later, now ravaged by hunger, the escapees were heading toward the Bezkyd Mountains. On the way they misjudged the distance to the town of Bielsko, whose lights they saw in the distance. When the lights of the town went out, instead of skirting the area, they found themselves in the heart of it, confused as to the way out. Knowing they might run into a patrol of armed militia at any moment, they hid out until dawn. Only then did they risk knocking on the door of one of the homes, hoping it would be that of a friendly Polish family. They greeted the older woman who opened the door with a traditional Polish greeting, "Praise be to the name Christ." She replied, "May his name be praised for ever, amen. Please come in gentlemen." After feeding them breakfast, she told them they should not risk leaving in the daytime because German soldiers were looking for anti-German partisan fighters. So Vrba and Wetzler stayed the day, chopping wood behind the house in return for another meal, and left at three the next morning.

They weren't so lucky several days later when resting on a hillside just beyond a village they had been warned to stay away from. The sound of a rifle cracked, and a bullet went flying over their heads. Seventy yards away, a German patrol had spotted them. They took off running through snow under fire from the patrol. Wetzler dove behind a rock, but Vrba stumbled and lay still as if he had been hit. They heard the patrol leader yell, "Cease fire! We got one of them." With that, Vrba jumped up, threw off his overcoat so he could run faster, and he and Wetzler slid down the other side of the hill through waist-high snow before forging a wide, fast-moving stream of cold water.

The dogs with the patrol in chase stopped at the stream, giving the escapees time to get away.

Then they came across an aged, Polish peasant woman, not knowing if they could trust her even after she said she would send someone with food in response to their request. Two hours later, a boy showed up with a parcel of cooked meat and potatoes, saying his grandmother would show up later with a man who would help them reach the border of Slovakia. The man was eager to help, even giving Vrba his slippers to wear because Vrba's feet had become so swollen he had to cut his boots away. The slippers were all the man had to give, other than directions to the border and the times to avoid border patrols. The trip to the border took two days. The slippers held up, but two impeccably dressed Dutch businessman did not. They looked as if they had been rolled in the mud through a bramble bush. The peasant farmer they first encountered found them some workmen's clothes after Vrba and Wetzler told him from where they had escaped and the need to stop the slaughter there. After three days in the farmhouse, the farmer took them with him to the market to sell three pigs and to a Jewish doctor in town, who treated Vrba's feet. The doctor took them the next day to Žilina, where they met with Jewish leaders and reported on what became of the mainstay of the Auschwitz Protocols.[6]

Six to seven weeks later after the four men had shared the stories of their escapes, they had reason to believe their lives were on a new path. Krasnansky used official identity forms to change the escapees' names and to register their new ones with Slovakian municipalities. He then hired an expert to forge exact copies of the documents the men would need when asked for their papers. Walter Rosenberg became Rudolf Vrba. Alfred Wetzler became Josef Lanik. Czeslaw Mordowicz became Petr Podulka (later changing his first name to Ceslav while taking back his original last name.) And Arnost Rosin became Stefan Rohac. Wetzler recalled later that the papers were so good he could have registered to study at the University of Bratislava.

Ceslav, for his part, remained focused on stopping the transports of Hungarian Jews. He kept asking Krasnansky, who visited the apartment often, if there were any replies from the Allies to the transcripts he had sent to intermediaries in Switzerland. He also asked if there was any reaction to the testimony sent to the pope's representative in Budapest. For several days Krasnansky had nothing to report, but then one morning he told Ceslav and Vrba they would meet with Pope Pius XII's representative at the Svätý Jur monastery nearby. The pope's representative in Budapest had received the Vrba/Wetzler report in May, but thus far the Vatican had shown no reaction. Now, after reading the interviews with Ceslav and Arnost, the Vatican wanted to question the escapees directly. "The first overt reaction of the Vatican came around June 20, presumably after it had received the second set of the Auschwitz Protocols that were based on the accounts of Rosin and Mordowicz."[7] Such a meeting could make all the difference if the Vatican believed their accounts. Jewish leaders saying the reports were true was one thing. The leaders of the Catholic Church openly taking up the Jewish cause would carry tremendous weight—especially in Hungary, a primarily Catholic country.

Around midday on June 20, Krasnansky drove Ceslav, Vrba, and Wetzler five miles outside Bratislava to the Svätý Jur monastery of the Piarist order of priests. (Arnost, who was still weak, stayed back at the apartment.)[8] Krasnansky pulled up in front of the monastery, a medieval complex with a spired church, grand meeting and dining halls, residences, and lush gardens. Although it looked peaceful enough, Wetzler pulled out from his jacket a pistol, holding it by his side as they walked through a garden in full bloom to a gate. The region was heavily pro-Nazi, and someone with knowledge of the meeting might have tipped off the German liaisons with Slovakian police, whose headquarters was nearby.

Waiting at the gate was a priest from the cloister. He apologized that the pope's envoy was delayed because President Tiso of Slovakia had invited him to lunch. "Would you like to come inside and wait for him in the visitors' lounge?" the priest asked. Ceslav, Vrba, and Krasnansky followed him inside, while Wetzler stood guard outside. About an hour later, Ceslav spotted through a window a large, black Czech Skoda limousine pulling up beyond the garden where they had parked. Out of the stately car stepped the pope's special nuncio, Msgr. Mario Martilotti, a tall, handsome man who looked to be in his thirties.

When the monsignor walked into the lounge, everyone shared pleasant introductions and then went into a wood-paneled meeting room with dark-red carpeting. Around an oval table, Ceslav and then Vrba related their experiences at Auschwitz. Vrba, Ceslav thought, was acting foolishly. When offered a cigar by the papal nuncio, who was in the process of clipping off the tip, Ceslav said, "Thank you, but I'm a cigarette smoker." At the same time, Vrba grabbed a cigar from the box and clipped it, as the Nuncio had done, laughing as if they were at a party.

It was then that Ceslav thought that at nineteen, Vrba was acting his age, and not taking seriously the opportunity they had to save the remaining Hungarian Jews. Ceslav, who at the time was twenty-four, was sweating as he repeatedly tried to convince the nuncio he was telling the truth. Monsignor Martilotti indicated he was very familiar with the escapee's reports. He asked numerous questions and took detailed notes. But Ceslav felt the nuncio remained skeptical about their accounts of the atrocities at Auschwitz. He is listening to us, thought Ceslav, but he seems to have some doubts about what we are telling him. Aware the meeting had gone on for five and a half hours and the nuncio might leave at any moment, Ceslav tried one last gambit. "Monsignor," he said, "listen to me. Not only are Jews being murdered, Catholics are also, even people wearing"—and he pointed to the while collar on the nuncio's neck—"but the murder of priests is not like the Jews gassed in the ovens at Auschwitz." Ceslav then explained they are slain elsewhere, naming Krakow in Poland and several other Eastern European cities. He said he had learned this from fellow Jews at the camp and from a witness who had seen trucks arrive, day after day, filled with boxes that contained the corpses of priests. They had been shot to death and their bodies brought to the crematoriums.

"Mein Gott! Mein Gott!" the nuncio suddenly screamed before fainting and falling to the floor. When he came to, he told Ceslav, Vrba, and Krasnansky that he knew hundreds of priests were disappearing, but no one had known what had happened to them. He asked Ceslav, "What is it I can do in this matter?" Ceslav reminded him that during the hours they

were sitting there talking, thousands of Hungarian Jews were dying at Auschwitz. They were not brought in boxes like the priests, but rushed into chambers, gassed with Zyklon B, and after twenty minutes thrown into ovens to be burned. Having painted that grim scene, Ceslav urged the nuncio to send the sixty pages of testimony from the four escapees to statesmen in England, America, Sweden, the International Red Cross, and, of course, to the pope. The nuncio replied, "I promise you I will do it in the nearest few days."[9] The three men thanked the nuncio for his time and started to leave. Before walking out, Ceslav touched the nuncio's hand. "Your promise gives us new hope," he said.

A few days after the interview in Svätý Jur, the monsignor met in Switzerland with Roswell McClelland of the War Refugee Board, telling him of his visit with two recent Auschwitz escapees and his belief in what they said of the gas chambers at Auschwitz. Monsignor Martilotti also alerted Pope Pius XII.

In mid to late June, deportations of Jews from the suburbs of Budapest began. Another 200,000 remained in Budapest, but they would be gathered for deportation before or about mid-July in a surprise "lightning strike" roundup. Municipal servants, including postmen and chimney sweeps, would help local police and gendarmerie units, observed by Eichmann's SS, roust the Jews from their "Yellow Star" ghetto houses. The civilian-military brigade would then march the Jews to holding pens in a sports stadium and two open-air marketplaces for shipment to Auschwitz.

It would be a massive and complex undertaking. Authorities had not centralized the Jews in a single ghetto because they feared that such an arrangement would make it easy for the Allies to bomb only the city's Christian neighborhoods, allowing the local Jews to survive. Instead, in late June, Eichmann's SS and Freneczy's gendarme troops ordered Jews to move and crowd together in a checkerboard pattern of 2,000 "Yellow Star" houses and apartments on multiple streets throughout the city's fourteen districts.

The newly inaugurated mayor of Budapest, Doroghi Farkas, declared on June 16 which residential buildings, listed by street and number, would become "Yellow Star" houses exclusively by Jews. Christians living there were forced to move out and could choose apartments in buildings Jews had vacated. A Jewish family could bring with it all the belongings its members could carry or cart, except for domestic appliances. At their new address, a family of four was allowed to occupy only one room—unless it was smaller than twenty-five square meters.

The last day of the relocation, June 24, was a Saturday. Tens of thousands of Jews were marched through streets all over the city. They carried their belongings on their backs or hauled them in handcarts, wheelbarrows, or horse-drawn wagons. Rich and poor Jewish families were suddenly living together under the same roof. One Jewish woman, who had a maid, a cook, and a large apartment before the German occupation, later described how demeaning it was to be packed into a single apartment with other families. "This was the saddest that I ever lived through," she said. "There came into our apartment three families with at least as many belongings as we had. Dirt. Messiness. Small child. Three women and factory girls were directing the kitchen—and I didn't find my place in my (own) apartment. With Father I fled into the living room. We were very depressed."[10]

The following day, a resolution posted all over Budapest stated that the city's Jews must wear their Jewish star emblems at all times and could leave their houses only between the hours of two p.m. and five p.m., and only for medical treatment, cleaning, and shopping. When commuting in the city, they had to sit or stand in streetcars in the back section reserved for Jews. They could not step foot in parks or promenades. And at home they could not entertain guests or carry on conversations with persons across the street or through windows. Any hope that Budapest's Jews had of being spared the deportations they had heard were taking place in the provinces quickly evaporated. Men in Yellow Star buildings stood watch at night to warn their neighbors of imminent danger. Many residents were so resigned to the deportations starting at any moment that they went to bed fully clothed and with their bags and knapsacks already packed.

As the negotiations with the SS on the Jewish lives for 10,000 trucks dragged on, Budapest's Jewish leaders did finally appeal to Horthy to halt the deportations. They sent him on June 23 a list of the number of Jews deported from towns all over Hungary "with a three-word evaluation of the situation 'ALL IS LOST.'"

Horthy didn't reply. For months, he had turned a blind eye to the atrocities that were happening to his Jewish population. Now he was expressing dismay at the many reports of the cruelties inflicted on the Jews in ghettos and the inhumane deportation operation. A few weeks earlier, to save his reputation, he blamed the Sztójay government. In a letter to his prime minister Sztójay, Horthy said he had not been told beforehand of the unjust measures taken against the Jews and, therefore, was not responsible. He ended the letter saying that "to avoid especially cruel and frequently inhumane actions," the two men responsible for condoning and overseeing the excessive measures, State Secretaries of the Interior Endre and Baky, should be stripped of power. He did not say, at least then, that deportations should be stopped. And Sztójay merely passed on the message to Berlin. Endre and Baky remained in place.[11]

CHAPTER NINE

MAVERICKS TO THE RESCUE

The wheels were already turning on other missions that would eventually propel the reports of the recent escapees onto the world stage. If the Allies would not stop the trains to Auschwitz, Salvadoran diplomat George Mantello and British spy Elizabeth Wiskemann would try some novel ideas to end the slaughter.

On the morning of May 22, 1944, Florian Manoliu, a Romanian diplomat, was having coffee in the dining car of a train with a diplomatic pouch on his lap. It was filled with citizenship papers, money, and medications for Jewish relief agencies in Budapest. They had been given to him by his friend Mantello, a Salvadoran diplomat in Switzerland. Manoliu had volunteered to deliver the supplies to Budapest and to ensure that members of Mantello's family, including his wife, were alive and well in Hungary (The family's name was Mandl; George had changed his name when he became a diplomat.)

After switching trains in Vienna, Manoliu took another to Bistrice, a city in northern Transylvania (part of Hungary) about 250 miles from Budapest. There he hoped to find Mantello's family. Manoliu learned from an official that they had been deported by train to a concentration camp in the northeast just two days earlier. He was crestfallen to hear the news. But to avoid suspicion he replied, "Good. We must do the same in our country."[1] Manoliu found the upscale home of the Mandls occupied by a Christian family. All over town white flags hung from houses, meaning that Bistrice was *judenrein*, free of its nearly 8,000 Jews. Over the next few days, Manoliu hired a car and driver to take him to other northern Transylvanian towns, where he saw the same white flags hanging everywhere. But where had the region's Jews been taken?

He hoped to learn more by continuing on to Budapest. Arriving on the morning of June 18, he went to the Romanian consulate, where he knew he could confide in the consul general about his mission. Manoliu added that he had a letter of introduction to Miklós Krausz of the Jewish Agency for Palestine. The consul general directed him to Carl Lutz, head of the Swiss Division of Foreign Interests, which offered diplomatic immunity for officials of countries not aligned with the Axis. "You will also find Miklós Krausz there," the consul general said. That afternoon, Manoliu met Lutz, finding him sympathetic to the plight of the Jews and eager to receive the contents of Manoliu's pouch. Handing it over, Mantello asked, "Tell me what you know or think is going on with the deportations?" Lutz hesitated. "You better ask Miklós," he replied, referring to Miklós Krausz. Lutz then led Manoliu to the basement.

Down the stairs, Manoliu entered a large, crowded room, where he was surprised to see some twenty people, mostly women, clacking away at typewriters. "Those are citizenship papers for Hungarian Jews to claim Palestine as their home," Lutz explained. He introduced Manoliu to Krausz, who was looking over the finished documents and supplying the typists with new blank ones. But Krausz was as reluctant as Lutz to share what he knew about the Jews who had been taken from Hungary. The Germans had spies everywhere, whose job was to ensure that the imminent deportations of the Budapest Jews remained secret.

"I see you don't trust me," Manoliu said. He handed Krausz a business card and a message in Hebrew from Dr. Chaim Pozner, Co-director of the Palestinian Office in Geneva. Krausz was the Budapest representative of the Palestine Office of Zionist Jews, whose goal was to create a home in Palestine free of persecution for the world's Jews. Reassured of Manoliu's intent, Krausz said, "Your timing is good, although the news I have for you is not." He had just received from the Palestine office in Istanbul two reports, one of which was a five-page summary of both the Vrba-Rosin report and the Ceslav and Arnost report. It is believed that Rabbi Dov Weissmandel, the co-leader of the Orthodox Jewish Council of Slovakia, wrote the first summary. The second summary, called the "Hungarian Report," was a town-by-town, six-page record of ghettoization and deportations to Auschwitz of Hungarian Jews. It had dates and numbers of people taken. That information is also believed to have come from Weissmandel, who had contacts in the Hungarian rail service.

The next morning, Krausz also gave Manoliu a long letter he had addressed to Pozner, the Jewish leader in Geneva who had provided Manoliu with his letter of introduction to Krausz. It said, "Dear Dr. Pozner...I see no possibility of escape, as we have only a few days before us...." He ended the letter asking Pozner to publish his letter and the two reports "so that the world may learn of the cruelties committed in the twentieth century in so-called civilized countries."[2] Manoliu feared this was what he might find out. But still he was shaken and, with tears in his eyes, he embraced Krausz. Eager to get Krausz's information back to Geneva, Manoliu stopped by Lutz's office to thank him and went to his hotel. He separated the pages of what Krausz had given him and inserted them among diplomatic papers, to disguise them if his suitcase was searched, and headed to the train station.

Manoliu traveled the rest of the day from Budapest to Geneva, arriving at two a.m. June 20 at Mantello's hotel suite. Also there was Mantello's brother and business partner, Josef Mandl, two years older than Mantello and just as driven to save fellow Jews. They had heard the rumors of atrocities in Hungary and feared for their Jewish parents and extended family, who were living in their hometown of Bistrice. Mantello also needed news of his wife, Irene, and her parents in Budapest. His son Enrico joined him after the invasion, but Irene chose to stay in Budapest to take care of her elderly parents. Manoliu had met with her and her parents before he went to see Lutz.

As Mantello embraced Manoliu at the door of his hotel suite, Manoliu told him what he had learned. "Your wife and her family are well in Budapest. But I have bad news from Bistrice."

With a voice shaking more from emotion than exhaustion from his journey, he explained to the brothers that their entire family, some 200 members spread throughout the region, had been deported, most likely to their deaths. Manoliu also gave Mantello a brief note from Mantello's father-in-law. It was written in Yiddish and addressed Mantello by his Yiddish nickname: "My Dear Bandi!...You cannot imagine what we have to endure. I beg of you, do whatever you can. Don't delay!"[3] As the news sank in, Mantello resolved to save the remaining Hungarian Jews, including the rest of his family. Mantello told Manoliu he needed time to think of a plan to publicize the truth about Auschwitz. "Get some sleep, Florian, there is a bed for you in that room," he said, pointing to another chamber in his hotel suite. Mantello then proceeded to work through the rest of the night.

Needed were individuals with bold new approaches to convince a wider audience about the truth of the Holocaust. Mantello, who was then head of the Consulate of El Salvador in Geneva, was perfectly cast for the part. He was well known among Jewish and Protestant religious leaders and the diplomatic community of Switzerland for his work in issuing Salvadoran citizenship papers to Jews in German-occupied countries. (See PROFILES for his background.) But now, with the news he had, Mantello knew that something more dramatic and urgent had to happen.

His first move was to put himself, rather than Pozner, at the center of the call to action from Krausz. He feared that Pozner would get bogged down in bureaucracy at the Palestinian Office and as a consequence would be too slow in getting news from the reports published, as Krausz had asked in his letter. So he replaced Pozner's name with his own as the addressee, figuring he could get the word out much more quickly. Mantello also changed the ending of the letter to broaden Krausz's appeal. Now it read, "Please use every opportunity to establish contact with all authorities and sympathetic people. We are certain that the Americans and English will help. Help! Help! Help!"[4]

Through the night Mantello devised a press campaign, the most important part of his plan. Switzerland, he knew, was the ideal hub from which to generate global media attention, as the country housed offices of every major international newspaper, as well as the influential Swiss press. Mantello caught a few hours of sleep before asking his secretary to retype the letter from Krausz, so that Mantello could use it and the reports to generate widespread press coverage. Mantello then enlisted thirty Hungarian students in Geneva to translate the reports from Hungarian to German, English, Spanish, and French. A few hours later he traveled to Bern where he convinced Freddie West of British intelligence to enlist Walter Garrett, a journalist with the British news agency Exchange Telegraph, to draft a press release.

Just before midnight, Mantello met with Garrett, who the next day prepared four long cables and a press release summarizing the two reports from Krausz and his cover letter. That evening, eager to get the news into the morning editions of foreign and Swiss newspapers, Garrett jumped on his bicycle with a satchel full of press releases slung around his shoulder. He rode through the streets, darkened by curfew to thwart air raids, delivering two dozen or so of the releases to reporters, editors, and radio producers. Mantello had told Garrett to slug the press releases with an Ankara, Turkey, dateline to give the media a reason to defy Swiss censors.

At the time such reports were banned because Swiss officials feared retaliation from the Germans. But at that point, having endured four years of censorship and with the sourcing of the news coming from another country, the editors argued that the authorities had no right to withhold the truth about Auschwitz. The censors backed down. By early July, more than 200 Swiss papers had published the story on their front pages, prompting Swiss-based diplomats and foreign news correspondents to call attention to the reports back home.

Mantello, meanwhile, lobbied political and religious leaders. He secured a mimeograph machine to reel off fifty copies of the reports and distributed them to international diplomats and Swiss officials in Geneva. The information reached political and religious leaders including US President Franklin D. Roosevelt, British Prime Minister Winston Churchill, Queen Wilhelmina of Holland, Archbishop of Canterbury William Temple, and Archbishop Francis Cardinal Spellman in New York. He also shared copies at an emergency meeting in Zurich he had arranged for rabbis and wealthy Jewish civilians who belonged to the Swiss-Hungarian Committee (SHC). Mantello and Josef Mandl had organized the group to help rescue Hungarian Jews after Germany occupied the country. After arriving by train, Mantello went to the SHC meeting at the synagogue of Rabbi Zvi Taubes, chief rabbi of Zurich. A dozen SHC members awaited him. Mantello read excerpts from the reports and Krausz's desperate cry for help.

The committee listened in shock. One of them, Rabbi Armin Kornfein, stood up and with tears streaming down his face declared, "This is like the destruction of the Second Temple," a landmark in Judaic history. He fell to the floor, and the rest of the SHC joined the ritual of ripping off their coat lapels while sobbing and moaning. One skeptic refused to join them, shouting, "This is nothing but Romanian propaganda," bringing up the old ethnic rivalry between Romania and Hungary. Mantello jumped to his feet and demanded that he be thrown out. "We've got too much at stake to listen to fools like him." The meeting continued as the skeptic stormed out.[5]

Before adjourning, Mantello told several members to reach out to government officials who were in a position to help. "We have no time to lose," he added. As for the original Krausz note to Pozner with his name as the addressee, Mantello asked Manoliu to deliver it to Pozner. But, either under Mantello's orders so he could get a head start or on his own volition, Manoliu waited two days, until June 23, to have the information delivered to Pozner. He didn't hesitate and aided the cause by contacting other Jewish leaders in Switzerland and the British and American consulates, as well as the War Refugee Board in Geneva, which aided civilian victims of the war.[6]

Mantello also had a plan to recruit Protestant leaders to speak out in the press and to their congregations about the atrocities at Auschwitz. One of Mantello's bolder moves was to march up the aisle in the middle of services at Rabbi Taubes's Zurich synagogue on the morning of June 24. In an infrequently used ancient custom of interrupting a service to convey vital information, Mantello approached the rostrum, rapping it with his knuckles to gain attention. "Please come with me now to see Pastor Vogt," he told the surprised rabbi. Before the rabbi could ask the reason for the interruption, Mantello led him out the door past a stunned congregation to a waiting taxi. They found Rev. Paul Vogt, a popular Lutheran preacher known for his work on behalf of refugees in Switzerland, at the office of his church. Mantello, who did not know Vogt well, wanted Vogt to hear about what was happening to Hungarian Jews at Auschwitz directly from his friend, Rabbi Taubes. "Pastor Vogt, please consider what our mutual friend has learned and what we believe is true," said Mantello. For Vogt, the news confirmed the rumors he had been hearing about the camp. Vogt quickly rallied support for the Hungarian Jews. Along with contacting the International Red Cross to provide protection for the Jews of Budapest, he and several other leading Protestant theologians were listed as the signers of a document Mantello distributed to political leaders and the press to urge Horthy to stop the deportations. At the bottom of the document appeared the names and cities of several prominent theologians, including Prof. D. Karl Barth, Basel; Prof. D. Emil Brunner, Zurich; and Dr. VA. Visser 't Hooft, Geneva.

Vogt had secured the endorsement of Brunner and 't Hooft, but apparently not Barth, an equally important theologian whom Mantello had added on his own. When Barth was confronted by the Swiss censors as to whether he actually agreed with what was viewed as an illegal statement, because of its anti-Nazi news, Barth initially said, "What are you talking about?" They then showed him the text, and, after perusing it, Barth replied, "Can't you read? Don't you see my name at the bottom?" Then he told the censors to leave his house.[7]

Around the same time, Garrett's press release and the Swiss censors' backdown sparked coverage in the local and foreign press. The first article appeared on Saturday, June 24, in *Neue Zürcher Zeitung*, one of Switzerland's leading international newspapers. Three days later, British readers saw the headline "Fate of Jews in Hungary. Massacre Begins" in the *Manchester Guardian*. Two Basel newspapers, *Thurgauer Arbeiterzeitung* and *Die Arbeiterzeitung* carried the same headline, "The Fate of Hungarian Jews," on June 28.[8] Those articles were followed by a bevy of similar reports in the American press, led by the *New York Times*, which carried two stories on the horrors of Auschwitz, one on the front page on July 3 and an editorial on July 4 titled "No Peace with the Butchers." The *Times* and other international papers had run reports about Auschwitz earlier in June but always on the inside pages. Many editors and readers recalled that in World War I there were similar reports of atrocities by both sides of the conflict, which led them to view such stories with skepticism. Mantello's press campaign, however, erased many of those doubts.

But was news of the eyewitness testimony of Ceslav and Arnost about the daily arrivals of thousands of Hungarian Jews, the Vrba/Wetzler report of the totals of Jews gassed to death at Auschwitz, and the letter signed by prominent Swiss Protestant theologians too late? The Jews of Budapest were days away from being deported.

While Mantello's campaign was leading to public outcry, Elizabeth Wiskemann, the British spy in Switzerland, devised a more clandestine ploy. Under the cover of a press attaché, she charmed many a diplomat and journalist for information she would pass on to the Allies. In mid-June, Wiskemann turned to Allen Dulles, the Bern-based head of civilian and military US intelligence at the OSS. Her office had received both the Mordowicz/Rosin and the Vrba/Wetzler reports from the Czech official Jaromir Kopecky. After forwarding them to London, she asked Dulles to send the reports to his American counterparts. Dulles contacted Roswell McClelland, head of America's War Refugee Board in Geneva, who passed them on to Washington.

One afternoon in late June, Wiskemann huddled in a meeting with her bosses at the British legation in Bern. They were debating how to respond to a request for assistance from Richard Lichtheim, the Geneva-based head of the Jewish Agency for Palestine. Having just received the reports of the four escapees from Kopecky and other information, Lichtheim had asked the legation to cable what he called an urgent message to the Foreign Office in London. It was needed, he said, because more and more reports were coming in about the awful fate of the Hungarian Jews and the mass murders committed by the Germans.

Among Lichtheim's suggestions to help stop the Hungarian Holocaust was a repeat of earlier proposals to bomb the rail lines that led to the camp. But, as members of the legation prepared the cable, Wiskemann, one of the few women to hold British diplomatic status, had an idea. She suggested adding to the list a request for the Allies to conduct a bombing raid of the offices and homes of some seventy German and Hungarian officials responsible for the ongoing deportations in Hungary, including police and railway officials. She would send the telegram without the usual complex secret code, knowing that Hungarian and German intelligence agencies were attempting to intercept and read every communique coming from the legation's Bern office.[9] The telegram reached the Foreign Office in London at four o'clock in morning on June 27. It went straight to Foreign Secretary Anthony Eden, who forwarded it to Winston Churchill. Reacting to the staggering number of Jews from Hungary, Churchill told Eden, "I am entirely in accord with making the biggest outcry possible." Nonetheless, Britain took no military action to stop the deportations.

But, thanks to Wiskemann's contact with Dulles, he passed on the same information to McClelland in late June that was intended to be intercepted by Hungarian intelligence. This time McClelland's telegram to Washington, like Lichtheim's, included the five-page summary of the four escapees' reports from Krausz to Mantello and the loosely encrypted, open-to-interception, list of seventy offices and homes to be targeted in Budapest.[10] Though it is not known who compiled the list of names, the War Refugee Board's McClelland, possibly with the help of Wiskemann and other resources, was most likely the coordinator. Besides his WRB role, McClelland also served as special assistant to US Legation Chief Leland Harrison. In June cables to and from Washington, McClelland and Harrison identified officials in Hungary responsible for the persecution of the country's Jews.

One of McClelland's telegrams relayed the pleas he was receiving for the Allies to bomb seventy residences and offices in Budapest.[11] It was one of three unencrypted messages to London and Washington intercepted by Hungarian intelligence in late June. Wiskemann's first goal had passed its first test, although she didn't know it at the time. Her hunch had been that Hungarian and German intelligence agencies feverishly working to crack the codes of the Allies would fall for a dumbed-down version. And when the intercepted news went up the ladder at German and Hungarian headquarters, leaders of those countries would know for certain that the Allies were now fully aware of the horrors of Auschwitz-Birkenau.

But, as they learned of the intercepts, would Hungarian officials really believe their days were numbered and feel compelled to do something to save face? As Wiskemann said in first proposing the scheme to her British colleagues, "What do we have to lose? It just might work." It was an American bombing raid that led to Wiskemann's ruse having its intended effect. She was a catalyst who, like Ceslav and Mantello, deserves more recognition for the end of deportations from Hungary. (For more on Wiskemann's career, see PROFILES.)

CHAPTER TEN

SHOWDOWN IN BUDAPEST

Early on the morning of June 27, two Hungarian intelligence officers arrived at the palace of Horthy on the Buda side of Budapest, high above the Danube River. They had called for a meeting with Horthy and Minister President Sztójay, who greeted them in Horthy's lavishly furnished office. Declining coffee, the officers handed them copies of a telegram and appendix sent from Switzerland to London that their staff had intercepted the previous evening and had translated into Hungarian.[1] "We are working on breaking the codes for several similar telegrams," one of the officers added. Dismissing them with a curt "Thank you," Horthy asked Sztójay to stay a moment. Reading the translations, each of them was surprised at the section listing the names and addresses of seventy German and Hungarian officials responsible for the deportations of Hungarian Jews to Auschwitz. "One more thing to worry about," Horthy mumbled. Turning to his minister president, he asked him to "let the others on this list know they have a target on their backs. And show them the news about Auschwitz in the telegram." Sztójay then left for his office in a nearby government building.

A few days later, Wiskemann's psychological ploy looked very much like the directive for an actual military mission. On July 2, more than 500 US planes dropped bombs on two oil refineries in Budapest, two supply depots, and a bridge. The massive bombing killed thousands of Budapest civilians.[2] None of the records for the five squadrons of the 15th Air Force, 459th Bombardment Group refer to the locations of the seventy persons on Wiskemann's list. But the bombs did damage office buildings and homes of some of those seventy officials. Ostensibly, the raid did not seem to be targeted at the officials or ending deportations. For one thing, pinpoint aerial bombing technology did not exist at the time. For another, the Allies had turned down requests even to bomb the rail lines to Auschwitz, saying that winning the war took priority over any rescue efforts. The fact that some officials' homes or offices were hit was more likely due to errant strikes caused by the cloud cover generated by earlier bombings of the city.

Still, there is reason to believe that ending deportations was at least part of the reason for such a massive strike. It did follow closely on Roosevelt's public warnings to the Hungarian government, the first at the time of the German occupation. The telegrams from Dulles, McClelland, and Harrison confirming mass gassings at Auschwitz led FDR on June 26 to issue an ultimatum to Horthy. The US would use "the force of weapons," FDR warned, "...unless the deportations are stopped."[3] In the wake of the July 2 bombing raid, fear spread through the ranks of the Hungarian government. The Allies, it seemed, were targeting them personally. Yet Horthy saw an opportunity for himself amidst the chaos.

Pressure on Horthy from outside Hungary had come in waves in late June. Less than a week after Monsignor Martilotti had interviewed Mordowicz and Vrba at the Svätý Jur monastery, Pope Pius XII sent a public telegram to Horthy. The letter of June 25 urged Horthy to "do everything in your power to save many unfortunate people...on account of their national; or racial origins...from further pain and sorrow."[4] The following day Horthy called an emergency meeting of the Crown Council at his castle. At the opening of the meeting, the regent cited the pope's and others' pleas before calling members of the government to end the deportations.[5] Horthy's motions were turned down. But he ended the meeting showing his fight was not over. Furious, he said, "I shall not permit deportations to bring further shame on the Hungarians! The deportation of the Jews of Budapest must cease!"[6]

Some historians have noted that the Vatican has not released any report from Monsignor Martilotti and the limited selection of documents it has released from the World War II years show only that Monsignor Burzio's transmission on May 22 about the Vrba/Wetzler protocol was not received in Rome until October. But that does not mean the Vatican was not informed on both counts by the third week in June. Secret channels of communication on all fronts was clandestine. According to David I. Kertzer, Brown University professor of Italian studies and an expert on the Vatican and its records, "The Vatican was highly aware that none of their correspondence and telegrams were free from the prying eyes of the fascist government(s). Where possible the Vatican used clergy traveling to carry documents or simply use such messengers for oral messages."[7]

Further pressure, resulting from Mantello's global press campaign, came in late June and early July from the leaders of neutral countries, including Sweden, Spain, and Turkey. They all sent telegrams calling for an end to the deportations. King Gustav V, who had ruled Sweden since 1905, wrote Horthy a letter chiding him for Hungary's treatment of Jews. "I have decided to turn personally to Your Serene Highness to ask, in the name of humanity, that you interfere on behalf of those among these unfortunate people who can still be saved," he wrote.[8] Horthy's family, meanwhile, also urged him to stop the slaughter. In late June, local Jewish leaders broke their silence, giving a copy of the Auschwitz Protocols to Miklós Horthy Jr., Horthy's son, an unofficial counselor to his father. Horthy Jr. showed the news of what the regent was sanctioning to his mother. Magdolna Horthy cried, telling her husband that when her neighbors and friends became aware of the atrocities, the family name would forever be sullied.

At the same time, unbeknownst to Horthy, he faced a threat from within his own ranks. Jaross, Baky, and Endre, the three government officials who worked with Eichmann and Veesenmayer, knew that Horthy would try again to get his cabinet to help halt the deportations. So the trio, with Veesenmayer and Eichmann's blessing, advanced the date of the "Lightning Strike" for the deportation roundup of Budapest's Jews to early July. Before then, there would be a coup to replace

Horthy. Baky came up with the details of the plan. The first step was for a gang of assassins to kill István Bárczy, Horthy's closest advisor and secretary of the Royal Council of Ministers, at his home. Then the gang would sneak into the Royal Palace through a passageway from Bárczy's home. Meanwhile, 1,600 trusted gendarmes would be arriving in Budapest to participate in a flag-raising ceremony honoring the heroic gendarmerie unit of Galanta, scheduled for July 2 at Heroes' Square (Hősök tere). Mrs. Horthy was to be the matron of honor. That was just a cover for their actual purpose of leading the surprise roundup of Budapest Jews for deportations. The plot unraveled at Bárczy's door at 10:30 p.m. on June 28. Just as one member of the gang knocked on Bárczy's door, another member of the gang got cold feet and killed the leader, and the rest of the gang fled. Still, Horthy lacked the power to fend off another potential coup attempt or to stop the deportations. He was only a titular leader within a government loyal to the Reich. And the 1,600 gendarmes, soon to be joined by another 1,400, were still encamped in Budapest to start the "Lightning Strike" deportation roundup.

That would change on the evening of July 2, when two Hungarian army officers ran into one another on the banks of the Danube in Budapest. The smoke from the US air raid that day was just clearing as Lt.-General Karoly Lazar, the head of Horthy's personal guard unit, spotted Lt.-Colonel Ferenc Koszorus, head of the 1st Armored Division of Budapest. They discussed the import of the attempted coup and the sudden presence of the gendarmes. Lazar told him that the commands of Admiral Horthy were not being heeded and if nothing was done Hungary would become a full-fledged Nazi state led by the fascist Arrow Cross party. Koszorus and Lazar saw themselves as patriots of Hungary loyal to Horthy and were determined to keep their country from being totally taken over by a foreign power. Knowing the risk he was taking and that he wasn't sure yet of the loyalty of his troops in such an endeavor, Koszorus told Lazar that if Horthy would give him the order, he would force the gendarmes out of Budapest. The next day, July 3, Lazar said he spoke with the regent who wanted Koszorus to carry out his proposed maneuver as soon as possible. Koszorus immediately gained the allegiance of his top officers and learned the gendarmes did not have heavy, anti-tank armaments or battle-ready personnel. Next, he drew up a plan to encircle and take control of Budapest with thousands of his well-trained troops. No one—including the Germans, the prime minister, the chief of the Hungarian general staff, or the minister of war—knew what was happening. In a few days, they were still planning on starting the roundup of Budapest's Jews to three collecting stations—the great market square, the pig market, and a sports ground near Vaca Road.[9] Horthy had called off the July 2 flag-raising ceremony, but the gendarmes stayed in Budapest "on leave."

The day before that surprise roundup was to begin, the two colonels in charge of the Budapest gendarmes were picked up at the Hotel Pannonia in an armored car by troops carrying tommy guns and taken to General Lazar's headquarters. He told them that Horthy had named him commander in chief of the capital and they and their gendarmerie troops should leave Budapest immediately.[10] To make sure they did, a few hours later at dawn, Lieutenant Colonel Koszuros met with his frontline officers at the northern edge of Budapest and ordered the sealing off all roads leading to the capital in case gendarmerie reinforcements were called in. Horthy's loyal troops were on standby just outside the city, with no fewer than eighty different types of armored vehicles.[11]

At nine a.m. on July 6, Lazar sounded an air raid alarm that sent the gendarmes seeking shelter. It lasted until noon, by which time the 1st Armored Division troops swarmed into the city, many concealed behind green branches in firing positions, while tanks and armored divisions moved into strategic positions. The gendarmes laid down their arms without a fight, and Koszorus's troops escorted them to trains to return to their home bases in the provinces.

While Koszorus's military plan was being hatched, Horthy continued moving on the political front to stave off blame for the Hungarian Holocaust. At nine p.m. on July 4, he telephoned Veesenmayer, asking him to come by right away. Veesenmayer arrived ten minutes later at the palace, and with hardly a hello, Horthy began a rambling dialogue that lasted two hours.[12] "I have to tell you that I just telegraphed the Führer to call back the Gestapo and restore Hungary's sovereignty," he blurted, followed by the non-sequitur, "I feel like a dummy without any authority in my own country." Then Horthy took off on another tangent, criticizing state secretaries Baky and Endre. "You should know that Endre does not act normal. Confidentially, two of his uncles died in lunatic asylums." By that time, Veesenmayer knew that it was Horthy who was not acting normal. Horthy continued his rant, noting that "Baky is a weathervane who was one day against the Bolsheviks and tomorrow might go over to their side." There was too much party strife, he added. "I'm not happy with Sztójay. He's as bad as Imrédy (former Minister President Béla Imrédy) who, you should know, had an ambitious wife."

Finally Horthy got to the point. He mentioned the flood of telegrams he was receiving from all over to stop sending Jews to Auschwitz, citing Switzerland, the Vatican, the king of Sweden, and the Red Cross. He hinted he would call for another vote of his council to end the deportations. But if it passed he wanted Veesenmayer's assurance that the Reich would not counteract it by calling in Nazi forces. Horthy hoped he could strike a deal by promising to step up Hungary's supply of troops and war materials to combat Soviet troops on the eastern front. "In view of the present military situation," where Soviet troops were gaining ground in Hungary, he said he "was prepared to do everything in order to combat Bolshevism together with Germany." Veesenmayer gave no indication he would acquiesce on deportations in any such quid pro quo, and hurried back to his office to telegram Berlin of his bizarre meeting.

The next morning, July 5, a day before Koszorus and his troops were in position to quell the gendarme threat, Horthy assembled his Crown Council for a two-day meeting. He knew that many of the ministers would be on edge, having learned from the intercepted telegram about the mass killings of Hungarian Jews and the call for pinpoint bombing of locations of those responsible. Opening the meeting with a reminder of the intercepted telegram and the bombs three days earlier that hit some of their homes and offices, he said, "I fear the destruction of all of Budapest might be next." Anxious council members looked at each other nervously. Sztójay wasn't about to let the prize of Budapest's Jews slip away: "We can let some Jews emigrate. But we must stay on Germany's good side and remain steadfast that deportations are only for labor." Horthy reminded him and the council that "the world knows that is not true, as we have seen by all the threats and pleas." He argued that the reputation of Hungary, which was the beloved home of the ministers, was at stake and that Slovakia and Romania had taken steps to stop deportations.

The debate among Horthy, Sztójay, and the council members raged for the rest of the day. When the meeting resumed on July 6, some sided with Sztójay to stay on the good side of Germany, allowing deportations to continue, while others suggested a compromise exempting Jews who had converted to Christianity or who had served in the First World War. When the vote was finally taken, Horthy won approval for the same proposal he had lost nine days earlier to end all deportations. With the army garrison loyal to Horthy manning the city, the council's vote gave Horthy the power to order an end to deportations. Lacking military power of its own in Hungary, Germany had no choice but, for the moment at least, to acquiesce to Horthy's demands. The Nazis had a scant several-hundred-man SS force under Eichmann's command in Hungary.

Minister President Sztójay hurried from the council meeting to telephone Veesenmayer the news. "The Regent [as Horthy was also entitled], in agreement with the Hungarian government," he said, "has halted the drive against the Jews." Sztójay added, in answer to Veesenmayer's immediate question, that

Germany could no longer count on the gendarmes or Budapest's civil servants to participate in the planned one-day roundup. "I must alert the Reich," Veesenmayer replied.

It is not known what the most important factor was in causing the members to vote in Horthy's favor. In Veesenmayer's lengthy telegram to Berlin on July 6, he cited several reasons for the council's decision, including Romania's and Slovakia's recent suspensions of deportations. He also noted the council's awareness of three intercepted telegrams to London and the US that referred to what was happening to Jews deported from Hungary and the call for target bombing with exact and correct street and house numbers of "the collaborators in this matter." Veesenmayer added that there was a further teletype that had the names of the seventy "main culprits" and that the intercepted telegrams "caused due effect" on the Council of Ministers.[13]

When Adolf Eichmann first heard from his cohort in the government, Endre, that Horthy had ordered the halt to deportations, he was shocked but saw it only as a temporary setback. Eichmann believed that Endre, as Hungary's official in charge of Jewish affairs, would find a way. But then on July 8, Interior Minister Jaross, under orders from the emboldened Horthy, dismissed both Endre and his other Jew-hating deputy Baky from their positions. Eichmann was livid. He rushed to the office of László Ferenczy, head of the gendarmes, to vent his fury. "This is the first time such a thing has ever happened to me," he exclaimed. "This won't do at all!"[14] Eichmann's cunning and determination would put Horthy to the test in coming weeks.

CHAPTER ELEVEN

A NATIONAL DISGRACE

The July 6 order to stop the trains leaving Budapest for Auschwitz came too late for several transports of Hungarian Jews from the suburbs of Budapest. They had departed the city just days before the decision was handed down. The vast majority of some 30,000 Hungarian Jews who arrived at Auschwitz between July 7 and July 9 were marched immediately to the gas chambers, small bars of soap in hand for the "showers" they expected to take. But the next day, there were no more trains from Hungary. The *Sonderkommando* Jews continued to receive transports of French, Belgian, and Dutch Jews in July and August and in August the arrival of nearly 70,000 survivors of the Lodz ghetto.

Eichmann, however, remained committed to sending trainloads of Hungarian Jews to Auschwitz, despite Horthy's order. The "bloodhound" snuck out a transport of 1,000 Jews from the Kistarcsa internment camp, near Budapest, on July 12. But after Eichmann's 150 SS troops stormed the camp, the camp's commander called the Jewish Council of Budapest. It prompted Horthy to command the Hungarian army to intercept the train and return its human cargo to Kistarcsa.[1] In retaliation, Eichmann devised a plan that would, in effect, keep the Jewish Council hostage while he again tried to deport Jews from the Kistarcsa camp. He summoned the council's leaders to an all-day meeting on July 19, at his headquarters in Budapest, to discuss what turned out to be a litany of mundane issues. The discussion went on into the evening, while all the telephones were kept out of reach. During that time, a train with 1,200 mostly Jewish men and women taken from Kistarcsa made it to Auschwitz. Five days later, as part of a similar plan, 1,500 prisoners from the internment camp at Savar, about one hundred miles west of Budapest, were also transported to Auschwitz.[2]

Horthy was livid. The regent instructed Sztójay to announce publicly that the deportations were without the knowledge or consent of the Hungarian government. Horthy, in another effort to preserve the safety of Hungarian Jews, later allowed the International Red Cross to oversee the emigration of Jewish children under the age of ten, if they could secure visas to other countries (a practice neutral countries were offering). The International Red Cross had taken a more active role in helping Jews in late June, after maintaining for years that taking sides in the war would undercut its refugee mission. Asked if the pleas he had received from church leaders and the criticism by the Swiss press had led him to change his position, IRC President Max Huber said that "pressure put on the IRC has been so great" that it intervened "just for the purpose of appearing to save its honor."[3]

The Germans, meanwhile, began work on a larger overall strategy to resume the "Final Solution." On July 10, Germany's foreign minister Joachim von Ribbentrop sent a telegram to Veesenmayer reporting that Hitler agreed to allow some Hungarian Jews to be resettled in Sweden, Switzerland, or the US—but only if Horthy would allow the rest of Budapest's Jews to be deported.[4] When Horthy once again refused the deportations, the Führer threw down the gauntlet, telling Ribbentrop to telegram Veesenmayer on July 16 that Horthy must be told that anyone who blocks anti-Jewish measures would be guilty of treason. More specifically, if "treasonable activities continue in Hungary, Hitler will act without scruples and with respect for Horthy's personal safety."[5] Threatened, Horthy tried a few stalling tactics that made it appear as if he was going back and forth on backing down. He replaced Interior Minister Jaross with Miklós Bonczos, who was just as anti-Semitic. He said deportations could continue but then clarified his position, saying Jews could only be transported within Hungary.

On August 21, prompted by reports that wholesale deportations out of the country were about to resume, five Budapest-based diplomats, led by Papal Nuncio Rev. Angelo Rotta, submitted a memorandum once again putting international pressure on Horthy. Two days later, Romania defected from the Axis and declared war on Germany, while Charles de Gaulle and the French army liberated Paris two days after that. In response, Horthy clarified his stance on deportations, saying only Jews considered by Hungary to be dangerous to the state could be transported beyond its borders. On one crucial point he was unwavering: he demanded that the SS and Eichmann leave Hungary immediately.

How would Himmler, founder and leader of the SS, respond? Would Hungry follow Romania and side with Russia? Germany still needed Hungary's troops to help fight the Soviets. Hungary also had oil, which could help keep the Reich's war machine running. To avoid a crisis with Hungary and prevent meddling by Eichmann and his SS, Himmler told Hitler that fighting over the remaining Jews in Hungary was not worth the risk of losing Hungary's indispensable oil production. Hitler agreed. Himmler cabled Eichmann and Veesenmayer in Budapest at three a.m. on August 25, ordering an end to the transports of Hungarian Jews to German territories, and directing Eichmann and the SS to leave the country. The "Bloodhound" did as ordered, ostensibly to receive one of Germany's highest medals.[6] Most of the SS in Hungary then went on leave in Germany, and Eichmann stayed on the Austrian border at the castle of Velem, as the guest of Hungary's László Endre.[7]

Emboldened, Horthy on August 28 took further steps to diminish Hitler's quisling government in Hungary. He replaced the government of Minister President Sztójay with one led by General Géza Lakatos. On October 11, Horthy signed a pre-armistice agreement with the Soviets. In return for Hungary laying down its arms, Horthy would be guaranteed autonomy for the Hungarian government. Horthy had planned to win approval from his Crown Council at a meeting on October 15. But the Reich had spies throughout Horthy's government, and before Horthy could convene the council, Germany lined up Ferenc Szálasi, leader of the fascist Arrow Cross party and its anti-Semite military unit known as "the Nyilas," to take over as head of state and minister president. Taking no chances, Germany launched "Operation Panzerfaust," rolling the 24th Panzer Division's forty-two Tiger tanks into Budapest on October 14. Ostensibly, it was to shore up the front line against the Soviets, but actually it was there to overthrow Horthy and those loyal to him in his army. For good measure, Veesenmayer lured Miklós Horthy Jr., the regent's son, into a trap on the morning of October 15. Horthy Jr. had been on his way in an armed escort to meet with representatives of Yugoslavia to discuss his father's armistice plan, which he and his wife, Ilona, had helped devise. But as Horthy Jr. stepped from his car at a corner in Budapest, the SS overwhelmed and shot Horthy Jr.'s guards. When Horthy Jr. resisted, he too was shot. Injured but not critically, Horthy Jr. was thrown into the back of a truck and whisked off to the airport, where he was loaded onto a plane bound for the Mauthausen concentration camp in upper Austria.

At the same time, Horthy was convening his Crown Council meeting. With the Soviets on the verge of full occupation of his country, Hungary had to break ties with Germany, he told the Council. It agreed and worked on the wording for a volte-face proclamation over state radio at one p.m. Horthy met Veesenmayer on a prearranged visit at noon to tell him of the armistice. Veesenmayer expected as much and came prepared. He urged Horthy to meet with Hitler's special envoy, Rudolf Rahn, to work out a compromise. Veesenmayer also warned Horthy that his son's life was at stake. Horthy went ahead anyway with the planned radio broadcast announcing that he had signed an armistice with the Soviet Union. While he was blasting the Reich for deceiving Hungary on many issues and maintaining that Hungary had not sold its soul to Germany to regain territories lost in World War I, German troops attacked the radio station, ending his broadcast. The station then read a statement saying Hungary was, in fact, continuing the fight against the Soviets. Horthy managed to escape to his palace, which had already been taken over by German troops, killing all but fifty of the guards. There he agreed to a statement negotiated with the Germans that his government would yield to the Arrow Cross Party of Ferenc Szálasi. He later said of his capitulation to the Germans: "I merely exchanged my signature for my son's life. A signature wrung from a man at machine-gun point can have little legality."[8] Horthy and his wife, daughter-in-law, and grandson were then deported to prison in Germany.

With Szálasi in power, a reign of terror began. The remaining fifty guards at the palace had their throats cut and bodies thrown into the Danube. Eichmann returned to Budapest from Berlin. His determination to kill Jews combined with the force of Szálasi's rabidly anti-Semitic Arrow Cross (Nyilas) Party, seemed destined to render immaterial Horthy's ban on deportations. The Nyilas takeover of the radio station set the stage for yet another wave of brutality in Budapest, with a campaign against the "Judeo-Bolshevik" menace.

The radio broadcasts touched off anti-Semitism that had been simmering in the city for years. Neighbors and coworkers looked the other way as gangs of Nyilas youths went marauding through the streets, beating and killing Jews for pleasure and anticipation of self-enrichment. The atrocities were so vicious, the new government eventually had to step in and inform the Nyilas gangs that it was the government's job, not theirs, to deal with the Jews. A few days later, the Vatican, Red Cross, and neutral states threatened to break relations with Hungary unless the minister of the interior, Gábor Vajna, reinstated the foreign protection papers for Jews that had been outlawed under the new Szálasi government. Vajna backed down, allowing neutral countries and the Vatican to issue tens of thousands more protective letters (*Schutzbrief*) and passports (*Schutzpässe*) than previously sanctioned by Horthy. Although the Germans would not let the Jews with protective papers emigrate to safe countries, the passes provided an extra measure of protection in case deportations to Auschwitz began again.

Around the same time, Budapest Jews lined up in droves to be baptized as Catholics, a joint operation involving Rev. Angelo Rotta, the papal nuncio in Hungary, and the Swiss, Swedish, Turkish, Spanish, and Italian diplomatic posts, as well as the International Red Cross and the US War Refugee Board. Rotta also worked neutral nations together to form an "International Ghetto" of several dozen modern apartment buildings in Budapest to house more than 25,000 Jews with protective passes.[9]

Meanwhile, reunited in Budapest, Eichmann and Veesenmayer planned a "new phase," as they put it, "in the solution of the Jewish question." Veesenmayer referred to it in his telegram to Joachim von Ribbentrop, head of the Foreign Office in Berlin. It included his and Eichmann's plan to deport 50,000 Jews on foot.[10] Trains increasingly were not available for moving Jews.

By the end of October, the Soviets had cut off most rail lines out of Budapest, Eichmann called the city's Jewish Council to his office on Sváb Hill to inform them of his plans. His face alive with joy, he said, "You see, I have come back. The government will work according to our orders.... The Jews of Budapest shall be deported. This time on foot."[11] He ended his remarks, rubbing his hands together, "Now we are going to work, efficiently and quickly. All right?"[12]

A string of death marches was planned. There would be additional groups of 50,000 Jews sent on marches until none were left in the city. When Veesenmayer informed the Foreign Office of this, Ribbentrop replied that the "severest" treatment of the Jews would be in the best interests of the Reich.[13] The first marches were short, to posts not far from Budapest, where trenches and fortifications were being built against the advancing Soviet troops. When crossing the Miklós Horthy bridge, Nyilas troops and gendarmes often shot stragglers into the Danube for sport. Then there were 120-mile marches to the Austrian border under the most inhumane conditions. Gendarmes shot dead Jews who became sick along the way or left them behind in abandoned agricultural sheds without medical help. Those continuing on foot were fed only a few portions of watery soup a day or nothing at all.

Early in November, Eichmann forced 25,000 Jewish male laborers to walk 120 miles in frigid rain toward Hegyeshalom, the Hungarian checkpoint at the Austrian border. Over the next few weeks, tens of thousands of Jews including women and children left Budapest in groups of 2,000 to make the same journey. At least 10,000 Jews died on the way. Those who survived would either build fortifications on the Austro-Hungarian border or be transferred by train to concentration camps in Germany. Eichmann was proud of his accomplishment. He later said, "I wanted to show these Allies my hand as if to tell them: Nothing will help; even if they bomb and destroy, I will have my way..."[14] Representatives of Sweden, Switzerland, Portugal, and Spain set out on the route to Hegyeshalom to issue protective passes to as many deportees as possible. After issuing several hundred passes, the Swiss delegation said in a report that at the Hegyeshalom border checkpoint, the conditions of the foot march "brought these pitiful deportees to such a state that all human appearances and all human dignity have completely left them."[15]

When Himmler learned about the conditions of the death marches, he summoned Eichmann to Berlin for a dressing-down. Aware of the renewed international outcries over treatment of the Jews and his continued concern for keeping Hungary as an economic and military ally, he reiterated his order of late August that there should be no more deportations out of Hungary. According to the war trials statement of Kurt Becher, Himmler's economic representative in Hungary, Himmler summoned Eichmann after Becher told Himmler about the forced marches. "In my presence," testified Becher, Himmler told Eichmann, "even if you hitherto exterminated Jews, you must now...become a nursemaid to the Jews.... If you think that you cannot do it, then you must tell me so."[16] Himmler, in effect, ended the "Final Solution" in autumn of 1944, most dramatically with his decision to destroy the gas chambers at Auschwitz on November 2. Mistakenly he had reasoned he could use the surviving Jews in Reich territory to bargain with Western Allies. After the murder of 40,000 Theresienstadt Jews at Auschwitz in October, concentration camp prisoners in general were to be kept alive as hostages. Despite those orders, the inhumane conditions caused one out of every two prisoners to die between January and May 1945, when the camps were liberated.

The death marches stopped, but Eichmann wasn't about to give up. His version of Himmler's command to "become a nursemaid to the Jews" was to establish an inhumane ghetto in Budapest for some 70,000 aged, disabled, and sick men and women, plus children who had not been taken on the marches. Eichmann figured it would be easier to complete at least this portion of his Judenrein campaign with these unfortunates in one small, overcrowded space. They would either die by starvation, disease, or some other method he would devise. In mid-November, the unprotected Jews were forced from their "Yellow Star" housing spread across the city to a much more overcrowded cluster of Yellow Star apartments. Nearly 12,000 Christians had to vacate the new ghetto to make room for nearly six times as many Jews. The ghetto encompassed only one-tenth of a square mile, bordered by a wooden fence. Nyilas guards and SS troops guarded each one of the four ghetto gates to keep the Jews imprisoned. Nyilas gangs of youths attacked, robbed, and murdered many of the Jews en route to the ghetto. Food was in short supply. Every person received three-quarter ounces of bread a day. The midday meal, doled out in communal kitchens, was thin pea, bean, or carrot soup. Disease was rampant.

Eichmann's biggest frustration at not having more Jews to lay waste to in his new ghetto was the more than 50,000 scattered in Budapest that were seemingly untouchable because of their protective papers from foreign governments, including Sweden, Switzerland, El Salvador, Spain, and Portugal. His consolation was from Nyilas gangs who assaulted them in their "Star of David" marked homes. The gangs also caused many deaths by blocking humanitarian aid of food and medical supplies.

Besides Reverend Rotta, two of the most dedicated Christians determined to help Hungary's Jews were Carl Lutz and Raoul Wallenberg. Carl Robert Lutz, tall, thin, and debonair, was head of the foreign interest division of the Swiss legation in Budapest. He was in the perfect position to help, since the Swiss legation represented twelve foreign governments at war with Germany, including the US and Great Britain. Lutz helped lead an international protest that reinstated emigration quotas. The 8,000 limit for Switzerland, under Lutz's interpretation, meant 8,000 families. And he surreptitiously issued tens of thousands of Swiss protective passes, overstepping his authority with the Germans and his superiors at home. Over the summer and into early October, Lutz and his team, which included his wife, Gertrud Lutz-Fankhauser, placed their protected Jews in seventy-six safe houses (*Schutzhäuser*) and in a former department store known as the Glass House.[17]

One day, in his chauffeured black limousine, Lutz saw Nyilas soldiers shooting Jews into the Danube. He screamed to his driver to stop the car and jumped into the river to save a bleeding woman. Dripping wet as he pulled her onto the quay,

Lutz turned to the officer in charge, claimed she was a protected Swiss citizen and demanded to take her to the hospital. The officer, not knowing what to say, shrugged and pointed his open palm to the limousine for them to leave.[18] Lutz's humanitarian work became so bold that Veesenmayer asked for permission to have Lutz assassinated. Berlin never answered.

An equally courageous advocate for Hungary's Jews was Raoul Wallenberg, a thirty-one-year old Swedish architect and businessman with Jewish heritage and a member of a leading Swedish banking family. He arrived in Budapest, on July 9, as an attaché to the Swedish legation but actually worked for the US War Refugee Board (with the approval of the Swedish government). On July 9, Wallenberg visited Lutz to learn the ropes for saving Jews with protective passes.[19] He quickly assembled a staff of forty that grew to 400, which issued up to 20,000 Swedish certificates of protection. Eichmann's SS and the Arrow Cross hunted him as he moved from one safe house to another in Budapest. They never found him.[20]

As Soviet forces encircled Budapest in December and January, tens of thousands of the Jews in the ghetto died from starvation or disease, or were shot and killed. Arrow Cross men (and teenagers) also murdered nearly 15,000 Jews in the cellars of Nyilas Party houses and on the Danube embankments. Along the Danube, to save ammunition, the Nyilas killers tied three Jews together at the edge, shooting the middle one in the back of the head so that he or she would fall forward, pulling the other two to their deaths by drowning. On December 23, when the Soviet army was closing in on Budapest, Eichmann fled the city, telling the SS, "No Jew must come out alive from the ghetto!"[21] He instructed the SS to get the German air force to bomb the ghetto, but the order was never passed on, as the SS force fled Budapest as well.

In Eichmann's absence, remnants of the SS and Nyilas officers enlisted German troops who remained after the Szálasi takeover. They would machine-gun to death all the Jews in the ghetto and in international protective housing. Surprisingly, Szálasi, the Arrow Cross leader whose Nyilas followers committed heinous crimes against the Jews, came to the Jews' defense, just as the artillery fire from the Russians could be heard in Budapest. Whether it was out of a guilty conscience or to look good to the conquering Allies is not clear. The stage was set for the mass murder by machine gun of all the known Jews left in Budapest. At the Royal Hotel, a force of 500 German soldiers and twenty-two Nyilas Party members had gathered with plans to mobilize 200 policemen to go on a murder spree that evening.

Fortunately, one of the police officers did not want any part of the murders. He ran over to the City Hall office of Szálasi, telling him the killings were about to begin. In the office with Szálasi was Raoul Wallenberg's liaison from the Swedish legation, pleading with Szálasi for protection of the Jews. "We need to stop this hideous mass murder plan," Szálasi said as both listened to the police officer. The leader of the Nyilas Party sprinted to the nearby office of the minister of the interior, Dr. Gabor Vajna, who said he was aware of the operation but would not prevent it. Szálasi then went to see German General Gerhard Schmidhuber, also at City Hall. Taking the legal advice of Wallenberg's liaison, Szálasi told the German general, "If you do not prevent this crime, you will be held to account not as a soldier but as a murderer."

With that warning, Schmidhuber called in the Nyilas Party member, a barber's assistant, who was to have commanded the entire operation; a German sergeant who was to lead the Germans; Interior Minister Vajna; and the police commissioner. "You are to prevent this crime as a result of my personal interest," he told them. Schmidhuber then arrested the German sergeant, and the others quickly acquiesced. Szálasi thanked the German general, adding, "The happiest moment of my life came when I was able to prevent this awful crime."[22] One wonders how he would portray the unspeakable slaughter Arrow Cross members committed under his leadership.

Soviet forces stormed Budapest, destroyed its bridges, and on January 18, 1945, freed most of Jews there. Budapest finally fell on February 13, 1945. In the prior three months, the Nyilas Party and Eichmann's use of Ferenczy's gendarmes had decimated the Jewish population of Budapest. An estimated 144,000 survived, "still one of the largest Jewish communities postwar Europe (excluding the USSR)."[23] But Hungary will forever be known as the sovereign nation that allowed and abetted the slaughter of more than 500,000 Jews at home and in Auschwitz-Birkenau.

CHAPTER TWELVE

RETURN TO AUSCHWITZ

Following the interview with the Jewish Council in Bratislava in early June, Ceslav was a wanted man on the run. After first hiding in a shared apartment arranged by the Jewish Council of Slovakia, the four escapees (Vrba/Wetzler and Mordowicz/Rosin) thought they would be safer if they split up into twos. Slovakia was still aligned with Germany, so they used forged documents and false names to rent their apartments with support from the Jewish Council. Vrba and Rosin teamed up in one apartment, and a few blocks away, from mid-June through the end of September, Ceslav and his friend Alfred Wetzler rented an apartment in the home of a Catholic family in a working-class neighborhood on the outskirts of Bratislava. Ceslav went by Petr Matusz and Alfred became Josef Lanik.

Although they knew their earlier, separate testimonies generated press attention on Switzerland and London radio, they believed a third report, written by all four was needed.

So they all met regularly in Ceslav and Wetzler's apartment to strengthen those earlier reports with personal observations and confirmation of the telling details of the concentration camp. The earlier transmissions did not record such impressions or judgments, nothing was passed on as hearsay, and only the tattooed numbers, not their names, were included.

The foursome began their collaboration on their new report after the meeting of Ceslav and Vrba on June 19, 1944 with the Papal Nuncio at the Piarist Monastery in Svaty Jur, Slovakia.[1] Sometime in July or August, they sent it to Jaromir Kopecky in Switzerland, the same Czech intermediary the Bratislava Jewish Council turned to for alerting the Allies.[2]

The Mordowicz/Rosin section of the Protocols contains some of the most vituperative comments, starting with, "All follows the most horrific phase of the Birkenau concentration camp. The apex, or bestiality of the Nazis, and their methodical destruction, an attempt to attain their destructive goal the biggest massacre and mass murders: The destruction of the (Jewish) citizens of occupied Hungary. We continue to work together to prove to the world about the depraved Germans. The animalism is now only reaching its peak. 15,000 killed daily in one Gestapo nest."[3]

To keep the family they lived with from becoming suspicious, Ceslav and Alfred left for what they said was work every morning at 7:30 and returned by 5:30. One evening their landlord's wife said, "Gentlemen, how nice you look; you are so nicely tanned. You must have an opportunity at work to suntan yourselves." They fended off suspicion by saying their jobs often took them outside to run errands and they would meet in the park to have lunch. Actually, they idled their time away hiding in the forest and avoiding town, playing the charade for several months. Just in case, Ceslav accentuated his Germanic features with a leather jacket and green hat with a feather.[4] "I may not feel like a German," he told Alfred, "but at least I look like one." They lived in constant fear of being discovered by the SS or Slovakian military. Ceslav always carried a revolver with him, either in a briefcase or at the ready in his jacket. One day in September, Ceslav and Wetzler took the train to Nitra, a city in western Slovakia at the foot of the Zobor Mountain, where Wetzler had a brother and family. En route, they stood at opposite ends of the crowded car—a move that would at least give the other time to get away in case one of them was stopped and held by guards.

"Document control," a Slovakian soldier said upon entering the car. Ceslav tensed, thinking he might have to use the revolver in his briefcase in case his new ID was not believed. Beside him stood a heavy man who told the guard he did not have ID papers since he was a German. When the soldier took Ceslav's ID and looked at its picture, he turned to the heavyset man without papers and said, "This is what you need, the real thing." Ceslav nodded to Wetzler across the car that everything was all right. When they arrived in Nitra, they slept in the train station because of a curfew; then, shortly before dawn, they set out to find the brother's apartment. As they took a walk in the park, waiting for the city to come to life, Ceslav moved his revolver to his pocket, just in case. All of a sudden, from behind a large tree, two Slovakian policemen appeared. One was short and chubby, the other blond, tall, and thin. "Good

Morning," said Alfred in his native Slovakian—not a language known to Ceslav. "What are you doing out here so early?" one of the police asked as he inspected their papers. The two said they were clerks from Bratislava who had come on the early train to visit friends.

The guards grew suspicious and refused to give back the IDs. "You'll get them back after we go to the office to check them out," the one in authority said. Unholstering his pistol, he ordered the men to begin walking toward the town square, saying, "If you make one step to get away, we will shoot you without mercy. This is a time of war." As they walked ahead of their guards, Ceslav whispered to Alfred in French, "We go to this corner, not one step more." Ceslav then put his hand on the revolver in the pocket of his trench coat. At the corner he pulled out the gun and fired a shot in the air. That panicked the guards, who dropped their guns.

Ceslav took off in one direction, Wetzler the other. "Capture the partisan!" yelled one of the guards, using the term given to Slovakian resistance fighters. Ceslav started running through town, around a winding street, and up a hill toward a monastery. The shouts brought people out of their homes, the police station, and the town hall to see what was going on. Ceslav raced by them, throwing off his trench coat to change his appearance. He ran into the monastery, which fortunately was full with morning worshipers. Kneeling down, he plotted his next move. Ceslav spotted the stairs to a bell tower and slid out of his pew. He would take refuge on the scaffolding surrounding the bell until church let out. Slowly pulling the rope so as not to ring the large bell, he used it to climb to the top. There, standing legs akimbo on either side of the bell, he waited. And waited. His legs screamed in pain. At the end of mass, the bells pealed and Ceslav's ears ached. But the bellringer below had not spotted him, and when he was gone, Ceslav climbed down and walked slowly toward the train station.

Suddenly, loudspeakers echoed throughout the town. "This morning at six a.m. two dangerous partisans attacked our city." The speaker then gave a description of the two resistance fighters and asked locals to help capture them. Ceslav picked up a newspaper, thrust it open in front of his face and pretended to read as he walked toward the train station. There, he was told, "Because of the latest political development, the trains will not stop here today." Knowing he could not stay in Nitra without papers, Ceslav walked fifteen miles to Leopoldov, the next rail stop, where he caught a train. After an uneventful trip, back at the apartment in Bratislava, Ceslav implored Vrba to search for his fellow escapee Alfred

Vrba took the train to Nitra, taking with him new identification papers supplied by the Jewish Council. When Alfred and Ceslav separated while they were being chased by the police a few days earlier, Alfred had gone to his brother's apartment. "Is Alfred OK?" Vrba asked when he showed up at the brother's door. "We are hiding him in a cabin in the mountains," he told Vrba. "My wife can take you there. It will be less suspicious than the two of us." After climbing an hour they found Alfred in the cabin. Vrba handed him the new identification papers, saying, "Now we have to get you back. They're still looking for you in Nitra." Fortunately, the police only had a vague physical description to go on, and when they checked his papers at the Nitra train station, he was allowed to travel on to Bratislava.

Not long after the incident in Nitra, in early October, Alfred's brother and his family left Nitra for Bratislava, where it was less likely they would be discovered as Jewish. One morning as Ceslav and Alfred were helping his sister-in-law hunt for an apartment, Alfred left them for a moment to buy cigarettes. All of a sudden a thin man in civilian clothes appeared inside the shop. He flashed a secret service police card showing he was an agent of the notoriously cruel Slovak fascist party Hlinka Guard, which was aligned with Germany. The agent then said he was taking Ceslav and Alfred's sister-in-law to the party's headquarters for questioning, as he suspected the woman was a Jew. Ceslav demanded that they first be allowed to have breakfast. "Alright," the agent said, "but my colleague will go with you."

The colleague, a uniformed SS soldier with a carbine, followed them into a cafe. Ceslav, who was a regular customer there, whispered to the cashier as he passed by, "Listen, in a moment Fredo (Alfred) may come here. Warn him that he should not come inside." Then Ceslav bolted for the rear exit through the kitchen, with the soldier in pursuit. But the rear door was locked. The soldier told him, "If you try that again I will shoot you without mercy," and led him out of the cafe. As he was being walked to the headquarters of Hlinka Gard, Ceslav attempted again to escape. As the entrance door was held for him, he slammed it back against the soldier and started running toward the president's palace.

That turned out to be a mistake, as the palace was heavily guarded. When the soldier pursuing Ceslav couldn't get a clear shot at him in the winding streets, he shouted for help. Ceslav ran down a street toward a gate but found it was locked. As he turned around, he saw hundreds of uniformed policemen and soldiers running toward him from the other end of the street. As the mob encircled him, many of them stepped forward to punch and kick the cowering Ceslav. He passed out and came to in a puddle of water and his own blood. He was in the cellar of the Hlinka Guard headquarters. Guards dragged him to a room on the first floor, and for the next three days and nights, guards hit him with shovels and large military belt buckles, until every inch of his body was covered with black and blue contusions. The Slovak political police suspected him of being a Russian spy, because he had attempted to escape and his answers to the multitude of questions did not add up. Finally, Ceslav came clean, murmuring, "I can't take this anymore. I am an ordinary Jew who is hiding from the Germans." Not knowing what to do with him, the guards dropped him down the stairs to the cellar where Ceslav lay dazed for a long time, without a drop of water, and hardly able to breathe.

The political police then hauled Ceslav back to the bare-bones interrogation room. It had enough space for a wooden table for questioning and an open area for kicking and beating prisoners. Ceslav was eager to cooperate, repeating that he was simply a Jew. "Look at me," he said as he unbuttoned and dropped his pants. "I'm circumcised." The officers laughed, and one of them said, "This is the first time since we began rounding up Jews that someone volunteers to be one of them. He must be crazy or else he is a Russian spy. Let's see what he really is." They ordered him to take off all his clothes, but he left his shirt hanging on his left arm to keep them from seeing the Auschwitz number tattooed on his forearm. "Can I put my clothes back on now. I'm cold," he hurriedly said after they inspected his genitals. Convinced he was a Jew, they took him to a holding area with other Jews awaiting deportation.

Slovakia had resumed deportations after a brief hiatus due to the Jewish Council paying a ransom to a Nazi official. Two days later, Ceslav was once again on a transport train bound for a concentration camp. He didn't know where until it stopped at small town in eastern Slovakia named Sered, where there was one of the hundreds of small Nazi labor camps. Ceslav considered himself lucky. It was not Auschwitz. But his relief didn't last long. He spent a night at the camp and was taken the next morning back to the rail station. The Reich was constantly moving prisoners from one camp to another depending on which camp needed more labor. "Wait here," a guard ordered Ceslav and the other prisoners from Sered who were crowding the platform. Five minutes later, a train with overcrowded cattle cars filled with Jews pulled into the station. Some were let out and marched off to the camp. Ceslav and his crowd were told to take their places in the now vacant cattle car.

"Please, where are we now headed?" Ceslav asked the guard who shoved him into the car. The word "Auschwitz" sent a chill through Ceslav's body and his mind raced. When the door slammed shut, he shouted to get the attention of his fellow passengers. "Listen! You are going to your deaths. I know this place Auschwitz because I escaped from there three months ago. They will kill me when I return, and they will do the same to you in the gas chambers." Some of those in the car shrieked in horror, while others stood mute, with a confused look on their faces. The train was moving, but slow enough to jump from and survive if Ceslav could convince them to put their combined strength into prying the door open. But instead of following his suggestion and jumping to freedom, people started shouting, "Shut up. You will get us shot!" They began banging on the doors, calling the German guards. Some jumped on him, beating him as if their lives depended on it.

Three or four men in the car believed what Ceslav said, one of whom knew him in Bratislava that summer.[5] They tried to help him, pulling off his attackers and making their way through the crowded car toward the door. But as they pushed and shoved, the angry mob forced them back and made them lie down on the floor. As he fell to his knees, Ceslav thought, The only thing left at my disposal are my own teeth. So, to avoid detection at Auschwitz, he slowly began gnawing away at the tattoo on his arm. Within the next two hours, with the peaceful countryside flashing through the wooden slats of the cattle car, an enormous wound filled with pus appeared on Ceslav's left arm. He moaned with pain and dread as the train approached Auschwitz. Ceslav had only one plan left as his train pulled into the new ramp leading to the gas chambers at Auschwitz-Birkenau. If the SS doctor who usually made the selection at the terminal was there, Ceslav knew he would be recognized. Ceslav would grab for the pistol in the doctor's holster, shoot him, and then kill himself.

As he stepped off the train, he immediately recognized the barking of the German shepherds and the shouts of the machine gun–toting SS to hurry and form a line. Nothing had changed in the five months he had been gone. Knowing that these were likely the last moments of his life, Ceslav joined the line for selection. A sudden peace came over him, as he knew exactly what he would do next.

Just then a hand rested upon his shoulder. "I know you well," said a man's voice. Ceslav spun around, expecting to see a guard who had recognized him. Instead, he saw a childhood friend who had lived near his hometown of Mława. The man was now at Auschwitz, tasked with unloading baggage from the rail cars. "I have been observing you for the last several minutes and I can see that you want to do something here," said the friend. "Don't do anything. You will get out of here, with my help and the help of some friends, and the SS will never know you were even here." Amidst the crowd confusion, Ceslav followed him step-by-step as they bypassed the selection process and ended up with the group of prisoners selected for labor. Ceslav and the men were marched off the rail ramp, around the back of Gas Chamber/Crematorium 111, past a wooded area and the main camp to the sauna/bathhouse where they were to receive their tattoos. Ceslav feared that the chewed out area of his left arm would be suspicious. "Follow me," the friend said, as he took him to a tattooist he knew would help. Ceslav came away with a new number surrounded by a fish shape tattooed around his raw wound. When historian Martin Gilbert first met Ceslav for an interview after the war, Ceslav said, "I suppose you want to see the fish."[6]

After Ceslav took the standard disinfecting bath in the next building and received his prison clothes, his friend took him to a barracks. There, another Slovakian prisoner who was the clerk gave Ceslav a pair of dark glasses for a disguise and told him he would count him as sick the next morning so he would not have to go out on the labor detail. Two days later, two prisoners who knew Ceslav from his first incarceration at Auschwitz led him to a gate where a train was waiting. "From this moment on your name is Peter Reichmann," said one of them. "You are from Slovakia, and you are going with a transport of fifty other Slovak prisoners to a labor camp in Germany." The next day they arrived at a camp in Friedland, in central Germany.

With only 500 prisoners, most of whom went out of the camp every day to work in the area, Ceslav began plotting his escape. For the next six months, he left the camp in the morning to work in a furniture factory watched over by camp guards. There, he befriended a fellow worker, not a prisoner, from Scandinavia. The man kept Ceslav posted on reports and rumors from the battlefront and how close the Russians were to taking over Friedland. Ceslav figured the Germans would kill all the prisoners before surrendering. So he would make his escape just before that was inevitable and when many of the camp's guards were helping the German army with a last-ditch defense. Ceslav's Scandinavian friend gave him food and cigarettes and, when Ceslav asked, a revolver. They packed it in a secret compartment of a large thermos bottle that Ceslav took back to the camp to be part of his escape kit, which included insulated pliers. Then, one day in May 1945, after overhearing guards say the Russians were closing in on Friedland, Ceslav asked four friends at the camp if they wanted to escape with him. "I did it once and can do it again," Ceslav said. They agreed to join him.

The camp was not well fortified like Auschwitz, and as Ceslav had expected, many of the guards had been redeployed to the front. Using the insulated gloves he had stolen from the officers' supply room, Ceslav cut through and short-circuited the electrified barbed wire fence surrounding the barracks one evening in early May 1945. He didn't need to use his revolver to get by the meagerly manned guard posts on the perimeter. Instead, he and his friends boldly started speaking a few Russian words they knew, accentuating them with "Hurrahs" as if the guards had already fled. The guards at the two posts nearest the Ceslav contingent fell for it and ran off.

With that, Ceslav and his fellow escapees walked out and found a secluded spot on a hill in the woods overlooking a road several miles beyond the camp. Friedland was 210 miles from Berlin, and Ceslav figured the Russian army would be heading through Friedland. They hid out there for three days and, as expected, saw a phalanx of Russian soldiers marching down the road one morning. Ceslav scrambled down the hill and waved to a Cossack on a horse, offering him bread and salt when he stopped. "Are there German soldiers nearby?" the Cossack asked in German. "Ahead a few miles you will find a few guarding a concentration camp," Ceslav replied. That afternoon the Russians liberated the camp before any action was taken against the remaining prisoners. After nearly six years on the run from and imprisoned by the Germans, Ceslav was once again a free man.

Without a family to return to in Poland, he sought out the only family he knew—his fellow escapees Wetzler, Rosin, and Vrba. He found them in Bratislava where the trio celebrated his return. There they lived together for a few months until they decided it was time for each to start a new life. As survivors they knew it wouldn't be easy. Memories would haunt them. For Ceslav they would include the first time he saw "*Oświęcim*" as his train pulled into the camp in December 1942. Forty-three years later, he said, "I'll never forget that sign as long as I live."

EPILOGUE

Now what am I going to do? Ceslav wondered as he enjoyed his freedom from the concentration camp in Friedland, Germany, when the war ended. The answer turned out to be working as a clerk at a large electronics company in Bratislava and attending night school for a degree in economics at Komenského University. Ceslav had an apartment in the old city center where many Jewish survivors lived and congregated on weekends. A young dressmaker, Ester Golubowicz, also lived there, and they met one weekend. By then, Ceslav had gained back the weight he had lost during the war and was once again a handsome young man. He and Ester soon learned they had suffered through similar traumas. Not only had both of them spent years in Nazi concentration camps, they also had lost their spouses at the camps.

Ester and Ceslav married in Bratislava in 1948. The next year, in April 1949, Vrba (whose nickname was Rudi) married his childhood friend, Gerta Sidonova, at Vrba's mother's apartment in Bratislava. There, Rudi reunited with his escapee friends from

Courtesy of Dagmar Wertheim's Private Archive

Ceslav Mordowicz (right), and Arnost Rosin retracing their escape route from Auschwitz in the Tatra mountain range between Poland and Slovakia in the late 1940s.

Auschwitz (Ceslav, Arnost, and Wetzler—whose nickname was Fredo.) The wedding party turned "quite wild," Gerta Vrbova (the female version of Vrba) later recalled.[1] Rudi "flirted with Inge (Gerta's friend) and tried to kiss her. He got very drunk."[2] To divert Gerta's attention, Ceslav took out his handgun and showed her how to take it apart and reassemble it. "I was not too impressed to have such a task on my wedding day."[3]

Rudi's best man was Rosin. "I sensed [he] had serious doubts about our decision," Gerta recalled.[4] His feelings were prescient. Their marriage was rocky from the start, with Rudi drinking heavily and jealous of Gerta's friendships with men and women. After the births of two daughters, they divorced. Gerta blamed the Holocaust. She was also imprisoned at a concentration camp and was the only member of her family to survive. "Perhaps at the time we didn't comprehend how 'damaged' we both were, and how it must have affected us."[5]

After their divorce, Rudi moved first to Israel, then to London, before settling down in Vancouver. Both he and his ex-wife went on to have successful careers. Gerta became a cancer researcher, while Rudi, who had earned his doctorate at a university in Prague, taught at the University of British Columbia and published papers on the biochemistry of the brain. Gerta and Rudi would meet regularly over the years. "After all," she said, "we had two children together and he was a very good father."[6] Rudi married one of his students at the university, Robin, in 1975. (Ceslav was not invited.) Rudi and Robin lived in Vancouver until he died of cancer in 2007. Robin Vrba co-edited an updated version of Vrba's memoir, *I Escaped from Auschwitz*, which was published in 2020. She declined to be interviewed for this book.

Ceslav received his degree in economics, and he gradually rose through the ranks at the electronics company, eventually becoming general manager of a sister company. The job came with plenty of perks, including a chauffeured limousine. The couple had a daughter, Dagmar, born in 1951. Their best friends were Alfred "Fredo" Wetzler and his wife, Etta, whose daughter Tatiana was Dagmar's best friend. Dagmar remembered she and Tatiana looking from the Danube River promenade near their apartment on clear days for the top of the 215-foot-tall Prater Ferris wheel forty miles away in Vienna. She also recalled how impressed she was by Rudi Vrba whenever he visited their apartment. "He was, what shall I say, a flamboyant personality who was very charismatic."[7] The last time Ceslav saw Rudi was in 1958, in Bratislava, when he stopped by to see Ceslav before leaving for Israel.

Seven years later, Ceslav and his family also moved to Israel, so that they could live openly as Jews. In Slovakia, under the Communist regime, it was risky to be identified as a Jew. Ceslav and Ester didn't even tell Dagmar they were Jewish until 1965, when she was fourteen, shortly before they left for Israel. Starting over in Tel Aviv, they no longer had the relatively privileged life they had enjoyed in Bratislava. Ceslav got a job as a shipping clerk on a loading dock and eventually became an executive with the Israeli army industry. Retiring at age sixty-five, Ceslav and Ester moved to Toronto in 1985 to be near Dagmar, who worked there as an architect.

By then, Ceslav no longer considered Rudi a friend. A rift began, at least on Ceslav's part, when Alfred Wetzler showed Ceslav a copy of *I Cannot Forgive*. It was a memoir Vrba wrote in 1963 with journalist Alan Bestic, which chronicled his experiences during the war. The book followed a six-part series Bestic wrote on Vrba's escape from Auschwitz in London's *Evening Standard*. Vrba had approached the newspaper with his story during the media frenzy over Eichmann's war crimes trial in Jerusalem.

Referring to Vrba's book years later, Ceslav wrote to Vrba's friend, historian John Conway.[8] "In 359 pages of this book he did not find a space to mention my name, not even once." Ceslav specifically cited the meeting with the papal nuncio at the Svätý Jur monastery on June 19, 1944, saying, "I am quoting from his book: 'The Nuncio was waiting for me—I had dictated my report in Žilina (Where was Alfred Wetzler?) When I spoke with the Papal Nuncio in Svätý Jur in Slovakia (Where was I?)'" Wetzler, Ceslav added, "in reality was the initiator, planned and carried out the escape from Auschwitz Birkenau on April 7/44.... All of the credit after the escape Mr. Vrba single-handedly took upon himself." Ceslav's partner Arnost voiced his bitterness in an oral interview with Israel's Yad Vashem memorial museum saying that Vrba's book is true, "except that he forgets to mention the others.... All of us who escaped for the same reason should take the credit for sharing in the informing of the world."[9] Historian Erich Kulka backed them up, writing that Vrba minimized "the role of Alfred Wetzler and conceal(ed) the escapes of Mordowicz and Rosin, who really experienced the murdering of (Hungarian) Jews in Birkenau which began five weeks after Vrba's escape."[10]

The rift grew wider in the mid-1980s with the release of *Shoah*, a widely acclaimed documentary about the Holocaust by French director Claude Lanzmann. Vrba was one of the survivors featured in the film. "It was all me, me, me, and also he treated Wetzler in a very diminutive way," Dagmar recalled her father saying after seeing the documentary.[11] She added that her father maintained that without the report he and Arnost provided, the end of the deportations in Hungary would not have been possible, and that Rudi should have pointed out the importance of Ceslav and Arnost's corroboration of the Vrba/Wetzler report. In the late 1980s and early 1990s, Dagmar regularly traveled to the west coast of Canada on business. While near Vancouver she arranged to see Vrba about reconciling with her father. Vrba by then was teaching at the University of British Columbia. "You guys were like brothers and didn't have anybody else,"[12] Dagmar said after they had settled into lunch at the university's cafeteria. She reminded him how they had shared an apartment while hiding in Bratislava, had remained friends after the war, and how all four escapees had celebrated Rudi's wedding in 1949.

"I tried to discuss the issues between Rudi and my father with no result," Dagmar recalled. "Rudi did not like to be challenged, and my father was extremely proud and considered it beneath him to reach out to Rudi. They were both stubborn, conceited, and affected by the Holocaust very much."[13] She added, "I believe deep down both of them had deep affection for each other but were too proud to reconcile."[14]

Ceslav did not speak publicly about his experiences at Auschwitz. He was not invited to appear in any of the documentaries about the Holocaust or to give testimony at any of the war trials of Nazi and Hungarian officials, as did Vrba and Wetzler. But, unlike Vrba who appeared in several Holocaust documentaries and wrote several memoirs, Ceslav received very little public recognition—other than interviews he gave for the historical archives of a few Holocaust memorial centers, including the US Holocaust Memorial Museum and Yad Vashem, Israel's Holocaust memorial research center in Jerusalem. In a YouTube video of the Yad Vashem oral interview in Polish, Ceslav cites the slights of himself and Wetzler by Vrba.

Asked to compare Ceslav and Rudi regarding their roles in informing the world about the Holocaust, Dagmar said, "My dad was not very vocal about the past. He had these expectations that the whole world should come to him for escaping Auschwitz and being the first to see and report the Hungarian Jewish deportations."[15] Rudi, on the other hand, she said, "knew how to market himself, which, in my opinion, is the primary reason for his ability to sell the story as he saw it." It helped, she added, that Rudi spoke English and, other than Rosin, who later lived in Germany, was the only one of the escapees who lived in the West. Ceslav and his wife only learned to speak English when they moved to Toronto in 1985, following Ceslav's retirement.

In 2002, Rudi made some amends when he published an updated version, entitled *I Escaped from Auschwitz*, of his 1963 memoir *I Cannot Forgive*. In a footnote, he said he did not mention Mordowicz in either the *Evening Standard* articles or in the original version of *I Cannot Forgive* because revealing Ceslav was Jewish might have imperiled his family in Communist Slovakia.[16] In the 2002 update, he gave more than a nod to Wetzler, writing, "My companion in the escape, Alfred Wetzler, was probably just as well informed as I about the events and history of Auschwitz and he could and did corroborate my data by his independent statement to Krasnyanski [sic]."[17] The reference to Wetzler was in a fifty-three-page appendix,

"The Preparations for the Holocaust in Hungary," written in defense of his claim that his motive for escaping was to warn the Hungarian Jews that they were expected at Auschwitz. Historians have pointed out that his and Wetzler's Auschwitz Protocol never mentioned anything about preparations for the arrival of Hungarian Jews, which did not take place until after Vrba's escape, and instead noted that the Vrba/Wetzler report did say, "When we left on April 7, 1944 we heard that large convoys of Greek Jews were expected." Esther Gilbert, the widow of historian Martin Gilbert, said in an email, "Sir Martin believed, based on Vrba's (first) memoir, that the Vrba Wetzler escape was to try to avert the destruction of the Czech camp (at Auschwitz)."[18]

After Ceslav's wife, Ester, died in 1993, he lived with Dagmar and her family in Toronto until his death in 2001. It was a result of complications after being hit on the sidewalk in Toronto several years earlier by a car that had mounted the curb. A freak accident was an ironic end for a man who survived Auschwitz, twice, as well as numerous perilous escapes and brutal beatings that would have felled a lesser man. But that is just part of Ceslav's legacy. Thanks to the Auschwitz Protocols, Ceslav and his fellow escapees (Arnost, Rudi, and Fredo) helped more than 140,000 Jews survive in Budapest. Hundreds of thousands of children, grandchildren, and great grandchildren of those survivors are alive today in all parts of the world, many in Israel.

Lately, some Slovak historians have pointed out that in the ongoing discussion on the creation of the Auschwitz Protocols, very little is said about Mordowicz and Rosin in Slovakia. "While Vrba and Wetzler are known, Mordowicz and Rosin are

Mordowicz family: Ceslav, Dagmar (daughter), and Ester in Bratislava, circa 1955.

almost unknown," says Dr. Ján Hlavinka, senior researcher at the Institute of History at the Slovak Academy of Sciences in Bratislava and executive director of the Holocaust Documentation Center.[19] He co-edited the 2016 publication of *Uncovering the Shoah: Resistance of Jews and Their Efforts to Inform the World on Genocide.* In their preface the co-editors wrote, "To this day, historians, but not only they, dispute when and where the information was received and how it was disseminated.... The proceedings of the scientific conference [in 2015] you are about to read is the result of efforts...to recall the heroic act of the two men (Vrba and Wetzler) but also to place it in a broader context topics of information, misinformation...; [and] stories of Arnost (Ernest) Rosin and Mordowicz who followed Vrba and Wetzler, successfully escaped from Auschwitz and supplemented information from the first pair." The 2015 conference took place shortly after the establishment of the Vrba-Wetzler Memorial and the first of what has become an annual seven-day march of 120 kilometers (80 miles) to commemorate the escape route Vrba and Wetzler took from Auschwitz to Žilina in Slovakia, where they were interviewed for what became the centerpiece of the Auschwitz Protocols.[20]

CODA

No one knows for sure why Horthy defied the Jewish genocide of the Germans when he did. Horthy himself did not reveal so in his memoir, although there is substantial evidence that he was troubled by the international pressure caused by the news about Auschwitz from all four of the April and May 1944 escapees.

So why then has the report by Ceslav and Arnost been left mostly in the shadows by prominent historians? It is reasonable to see why the Vrba/Wetzler report warranted top billing in postwar credit for recognition of the genocide. Their report not only had the shocking number of those gassed to death, but the details and drawings of how Auschwitz-Birkenau functioned. The catalytic role Ceslav and Arnost played in drawing crucially needed attention to the Vrba/Wetzler report has largely gone missing, however. That apparently is largely due to the fact that the War Refugee Board in Switzerland got several important facts wrong in communicating to Washington headquarters the Auschwitz Protocols. The WRB released the Protocols to the public on November 26, 1944, to widespread horror. The prosecution cited the three reports of the escapees in the postwar trials of Nazi officials. More than 400 Jewish organizations ordered copies of the Protocols, which made the front page of the *New York Times* and other major newspapers. It was "the most shocking document ever issued by a United States government agency," said *The International Herald Tribune* on November 26. The Protocols remain the template for the genocide at Auschwitz tragedy.

A close reading of the cover note Roswell McClelland originally sent the reports on October 12 to his boss in Washington, John Pehle, and the subsequent public WRB report in late November reveals the errors. It shows McClelland was confused about the relevance and timing of the Mordowicz/Rosin report.

Here is what was misunderstood. The WRB's document maintained that the report of two unnamed Slovak escapees (later identified as Vrba and Wetzler) on April 7, 1944, was verifiable. But, in referring to what was later identified as the Mordowicz/Rosin report, "it has not been possible, however, to check the origin of this report as closely as the first."[1] That was not so. As noted earlier in this book, members of the Slovakian Jewish Committee had interviewed Ceslav and Arnost with the same vigorous interrogation as that of Vrba and Wetzler. The committee brought all four together and cross examined them separately in early June after Ceslav and Arnost had escaped. The committee, including its chief interviewer and scribe Oskar Krasnansky, believed their reports were consistent.[2]

McClelland told Pehle that it was not possible to check the other report (that of Mordowicz/Rosin) as closely as the first, because "on August 6, 1944, a report was received in Switzerland [that of Ceslav and Arnost] covering the happenings in Birkenau during the period between April 7 and May 27." The August 6 date was wrong. Many historians reported that both sets of escapee reports reached diplomats in Switzerland, including McClelland, not in August after the deportation ban, but in the second half of June 1944, before the ban on deportations on July 6.

Another misunderstanding is seen in the cover letter McClelland sent Pehle with the Protocols on October 12, 1944, in which he (McClelland) said he had met with the papal nuncio who personally interviewed "the two young Slovak Jews...and declared the impression they created in telling their story to be thoroughly convincing."[3] It was Ceslav, a Polish Jew, the nuncio interviewed with Vrba, not Wetzler. Both Vrba and Wetzler were Slovakian.[4] Thus, McClelland mistakenly believed that the independent scrutiny of the Vrba/Wetzler information by the pope's emissary did not include the verification and additional eyewitness conversations the nunciature had with Ceslav.

As a result of all that confusion, it is understandable why the existence of the Ceslav and Arnost report was underplayed in the WRB document. Their report was only incorporated as a four-page addendum entitled "111" at the end of the twenty-eight-page Vrba/Wetzler report. But instead of noting the Mordowicz/Rosin Protocol as the second report, it listed the second report as that of the "Polish Major."[5] It is a sixteen-page description of beatings, torture, and death by lethal gas at Auschwitz that garnered little attention when written in late 1943 by its escapee author Jerzy Tabeau.

To be fair to McClelland, he was besieged with the work in 1944 of both leading the WRB's mission in Europe to save the

Jews and serving as special assistant to the US minister to Switzerland, Leland Harrison. When he met with or heard from Swiss diplomats and the Vatican's legate about the Auschwitz gas chambers, the focus was on the data and descriptions of the killing mechanisms depicted from the Vrba/Wetzler report.

Who gets or deserves more or less credit for helping to save the lives of fellow human beings pales in significance, of course, to the Holocaust itself. Ironically, the tally of Jewish and other victims at Auschwitz remained somewhat of a controversy for decades. Families, friends, and survivors knew whom they lost. But evidence at the Nuremberg war crime trials and other investigations ranged from 2.5 million to as many as 5 million deaths at Auschwitz. In addition to the Auschwitz Protocols, the sources included former prisoners and SS staff at Auschwitz, including SS physician Friedrich Entress. Rudolf Höss, Auschwitz commandant from 1942 to 1945, testified at Nuremberg in 1946 that 2.5 million Jews were gassed to death and another 500,000 died from illness or starvation. But at a second trial in 1947, he claimed his year-earlier testimony had been based on Eichmann's account of having overseen the deportation to Auschwitz of 2.5 million Jews and that he (Höss) had since regarded that as too high. Höss's own recollection of Jews killed at Auschwitz from major countries, including 400,000 from Hungary, was only 1,130,00. Still, he kept the higher number theory alive by stating in his final testimony at that trial that "millions perished here, but I am unable to determine the exact number."[6]

The discrepancies in death stems from a lack of official records. Only those arrivals chosen for labor were registered.

The rest of the arrivals, mostly Jews, were immediately gassed to death without identification. Höss destroyed his records at Auschwitz. For many years after the war it was commonly believed that 2 to 2.5 million Jews were murdered at Auschwitz, and the total death of 4 million or more continued to be bandied about. The Auschwitz-Birkenau State Museum did not conduct its own investigation until 1962 when a member of the Research Board said, "It is a task of the greatest importance... to set about attempting to establish an estimate of the number of victims of Auschwitz."[7] Until then, only a few historians, notably Gerald Reitlinger, 1953, and Raul Hilberg, 1961, had far lower estimates.

Further research by the museum and others revealed a far lower death toll, primarily because there was a lesser number of deportees to the camp from countries originating the transports than originally believed. Sources included German records that had not been destroyed and indigenous collaborators from occupied countries who had kept exact count of the number of deportees transported to Auschwitz. One study listed country after country with fewer deportees, such as 450,00 from Poland instead of 2.3 million. "All the (total of country) transports show that at least 1.3 million people were transported to the camp (Auschwitz) in the less than five years it existed."[8] The US Holocaust Memorial Museum now cites a figure of at least 1.1 million deaths at Auschwitz, of which at least 1 million were Jews. The Auschwitz-Birkenau State Museum provides roughly the same ballpark figure.

As for the number of Hungarian Jews killed in Auschwitz, present and past historians have always been on the same page:

More than 400,000 Jews died in Auschwitz, the vast majority in the gas chambers, or from starvation or disease. Still, at the end of 1945, alive after the war were an estimated 255,500, out of an estimated 825,000 Jews residing within the borders of Hungary before deportations in 1944. The survivors included 144,000 liberated in Budapest, liberated labor servicemen, and those returned from deportation.[9] The other 110,000 or so survivors were those who escaped across neighboring borders, lived under false identities, or hid underground. After the war, most immigrated to Palestine or joined relatives in America or England.

PROFILES

GEORGE (MANDL) MANTELLO was a Transylvanian Jew born in 1901 who used his fierce drive, uncanny intuition, and cunning schemes to become a rich businessman in Eastern Europe. More telling, he was a man not just willing, but eager, to take chances—a trait that would become essential in his drive to save Budapest's Jews. As a young man who dressed fashionably in tailored suits, he first worked at a Vienna bank, earning enough money to buy a textile mill in Bucharest in the early 1920s. He then went to work in his father and uncle's granary business, where he enraged both of them by speculating on a risky commodities deal. Having been delegated to buy one hundred train carloads of grain, he went behind his father and uncle's back and purchased five times as much.[1]

"You're going to ruin us," yelled the uncle after George broke the news. "We'll make a fortune!" Mantello insisted. He was right. The price of grain began rising and within a few months it was up by nearly 60 percent. But Mantello never got over the harsh criticism. He returned to banking, financing granary deals and speculating in currencies. Before long-distance phone calls became routine, day and night he was on the phone to

George Mantello, an El Salvador diplomat in Switzerland who approved citizen documents for Hungarian Jews and who led a press campaign that put pressure on Hungary's leader to end deportations of more than 200,000 Budapest Jews.

Courtesy of the United States Holocaust Memorial Museum Archives, Washington, DC, 2009.50.1 for the George Mandl Mantello Collection and Enrico Mandel

three operators connected to the foreign exchange markets in New York, London, and Zurich. He had hired them to report instantly on the price changes on foreign currencies in one market, which he would use to his advantage in other markets before other investors had even learned of the change.

He made enough money to quit the bank and try his hand at various business ventures, maintaining dual residences in Bucharest and Budapest, where he met his future wife, Irene Berger. Their only child, Enrico, was born in 1928. Six years later, Mantello and Enrico were on a bus trip to visit relatives in rural Transylvania when a tire blew out. While passengers stood outside the bus watching the driver change the tire, a bull burst through a wooden fence, ramming its horns repeatedly into the side of the bus. "This can go on forever; we can't wait," Mantello told the driver. As the rest of the passengers stood terrified, Mantello walked over to the bull, talked to it until it was calm, and led it by the horn back to its barn. Enrico later said his father was like that all this life. "The man had no physical fear."[2]

Giving Mantello a leg up on making business connections was his status as a diplomat. In 1938 he had been named honorary attaché of the El Salvador legation in Bucharest by José Arturo Castellanos, the Salvadoran consul general in Hamburg, Germany. By that time, George Mandl had changed his last name to Mantello, which sounded more Latin when pronounced: "Mantellyo." Four years later, in 1942, Castellanos named Mantello first secretary of the country's consulate in Geneva, then the diplomatic hub of Europe. Mantello set out to help persecuted Jews following business trips, in 1938 and 1939, to cities in German-occupied European countries, where he saw Jews being beaten physically, as well as persecuted by anti-Semitic laws. "I always saw before me heartrending scenes of the terrible Jewish martyrdom in Nazi-occupied Vienna and Prague," he recalled later. In the autumn of 1942, Mantello figured one way to "save my fellow Jews" was to form a Swiss rabbis' committee that would become, in effect, a lobbying group to Protestant theologians and Allied diplomats in Switzerland.

So, he approached local Swiss rabbis, including the chief rabbi of Zurich. They told him they would join a Swiss rabbis' committee if Mantello could overcome the objections of their titular leader, who believed rabbis should focus only on Judaic religious issues. The leader, George Brunschvig, said calling on Christian church groups and foreign missions to rescue Jews was a controversial issue to be avoided. Incensed at the road-block, Mantello telephoned Brunschvig and lit into him when diplomatic courtesy got him nowhere. "Don't you care what is happening to Jews all over Eastern Europe? I have seen with my own eyes that the Germans are criminals straight out of Hell," Mantello said.[3] Mantello's lecture softened the leader and those contacts would become essential in the coming years of Mantello's first notable achievements—the issuance of diplo-matic protective papers to Jews in occupied countries and a global press campaign to pressure Hungary's leader, Miklós Horthy, to stop the deportations of Jews to Auschwitz.

The protective citizenship paper scheme began in 1941, when a Jewish family from Poland, then living in Switzerland, learned their relatives could live outside the Polish ghetto and not wear the Jewish star if they had "proof" of foreign citizen-ship. The family offered Latin American consuls in Switzerland, including the consulate of Paraguay, hefty sums to issue pass-ports to the family's friends and relatives in Poland. Around the same time, Jewish religious leaders also learned of the loophole and began buying passports or citizenship papers, for 50 to 300 Swiss francs each, and sent them to Jews in occupied countries. A few of the global Jewish organizations declined to endorse the questionable practice. Just about everyone knew the protective papers issued to Jews who never had been foreign citizens were dicey or semi-legal at best.

But the Latin American countries issuing the phony papers, including El Salvador, had the one essential thing going for them—the Reich actually recognized them as valid for several years. It had several hundred thousand German nationals living in Latin America during the war, and German officials of the Foreign Office believed if they did not honor the citizenship papers "these states may take reprisals against Reich Germans."[4] If needed, the protected status of those European Jews with papers could serve as barter for German nationals in Latin countries. That might occur if the Allies put pressure on Latin countries to treat German nationals there as the enemy.

Mantello broke ranks with other Latin delegations by issuing citizenship papers for free or by simply covering costs to anyone who asked for them. To speed things up, Mantello sent papers signed and officially stamped directly to Jews in occupied countries where they could affix their own photos and fill in their birth dates rather than send them to Mantello to complete and resend. The first ones went to Jews in Belgium, Holland, France, Poland, and Slovakia. To convince Jews to use them, he made them look more official than those of other countries. Instead of a single sheet, he provided three-page documents in several languages, stamped by an official interpreter. Knowing the German officials revered ornate government stamps, he added one from Swiss tax authorities signifying the person holding the document had paid Swiss taxes as a good citizen. Germany's invasion of Hungary, in March 1944, drove Mantello and his staff to ramp up its issuance of papers there.[5]

Mantello's good deeds didn't end with issuing Salvadoran papers to European Jews or with his press campaign to generate attention for the Auschwitz Protocols. In the waning days of the war, he joined others in securing the release of a number of prisoners from the Bergen-Belsen concentration camp. A few years after the war, Mantello rescued Monsignor Béla Varga, the last president of the Hungarian Parliament, prior to the Communist takeover in 1947. Mantello knew Varga's life was in danger because he staunchly resisted Communism. In a hand-to-hand battle with a would-be assassin of Varga at a resort near Vienna, Mantello wrested a weapon away and threw him out the door. Mantello then enlisted the aid of the American OSS and Swiss intelligence to smuggle Varga into Switzerland.[6] Later, Mantello helped Israel buy armaments with low-interest loans. He died in Rome in 1992 and is buried in Israel.[7]

Elizabeth Wiskemann, a British attaché in Switzerland who purposely sent unencrypted telegrams about bombing the offices and residences of seventy officials responsible for deportations of Hungarian Jews to Auschwitz. An apparently unrelated American bombing of Budapest preceded the country's government to ban deportations a few days later.

ELIZABETH WISKEMANN, known to her friends as "Whiskers," had a nose for news, an ear for gossip, and an intellect to know the difference between the two. An attractive, petite woman with a charming manner, she held strong opinions that she was quick to defend when challenged. Driven by a fierce curiosity, she made her mark as a young freelance journalist in the 1930s, writing about political upheaval in Germany that led to the collapse of the Weimar Republic and the rise of the Third Reich. After receiving a master's degree in literature from Cambridge, she accepted a teaching job there that allowed her to take off every other semester to return to Germany on reporting assignments. When Adolf Hitler was appointed chancellor in early 1933, she quickly learned that the Nazi Party was using torture, propaganda, and fear to entrench itself. She saw Jewish ice cream vendors beaten up by police and civilians because the Reich had said not to buy from Jews.

Wiskemann was one of several journalists who learned, in early March 1933, that the Nazis had set up their first Jewish concentration camp for political prisoners. Later that month she returned to London and briefed the House of Commons on the threats to freedom occurring in Nazi Germany. Few lawmakers believed her accounts, and some even called her a "Cassandra."[1]

Undeterred, Wiskemann went back to Europe to report on the Reich. In July 1935, she published an article in the *New Statesman and Nation* that offered a rare and insightful look at life inside Hitler's Germany. In it, Wiskemann chided readers for assuming the Reich was benign, writing that "the maltreatment of the Jews is being carried to hitherto unknown lengths." She added that the liberals and intellectuals she spoke to in Germany regularly asked, "Can't you make your countrymen understand that we are fighting for all the values upon which European civilization depends?" She was convinced that Hitler was on the path to war. She noted that weapons factories in Germany had roared to life, and coinciding with the March 1935 German government introduction of mandatory male conscription for the armed services, contractors were busily building new barracks.[2]

Her reportage drew the attention of the Gestapo, which circulated an order that said, "It seems probable that Wiskemann will come to Germany again soon. Should this writer turn up it is to be reported at once without preventing her entry."[3] In 1936, Wiskemann returned to Europe to report on the Nazi

Party's attempt to win electoral control of the Free City of Danzig. When she stopped in Berlin on the way back to Britain, she was apprehended by the Gestapo and taken to its headquarters in the Prinz Albrecht Strasse. While awaiting interrogation, rather than worry, she said to herself, "Do, for heaven's sake, look around. You're in a place of unusual interest." Then, an SS officer asked her if she had written that Jews were maltreated in Nazi Germany. "Why yes, it's true isn't it," she replied. Next, he asked her if she had written that Nazi Germany was dominated by "brutal SS types," such as Himmler and Heydrich. Again, she brazenly replied, "Why not, isn't that fairly exact, too?" When the British Embassy secured her release, she informed them about the maps she had seen on the walls. They were of Poland and other Eastern European countries, hints that an eastward expansion was in the planning stages.[4]

In the summer of 1936 "EW," as she often signed her telegrams, was in one sense a journalist without a country. Her expertise and base of sources had been in Germany, but she was told upon her release by the Gestapo that she could no longer work or live there. But her fluency in German allowed her to relocate to Czechoslovakia, where she arranged dozens of meetings with government officials, as well as influential artists, socialists, and others keenly aware of the threat Germany posed to the rest of Europe. She wrote a book, *Czechoslovakia Prepares*, published by the *New Statesman*, in which she pointed out why Czechoslovakia was most likely on Hitler's hit list. Among the more obvious reasons: it could serve as a staging area from which German forces could attack Russia.[5]

British officials, impressed by Wiskemann's dogged reporting, offered her a job in the government's expanding intelligence network. Working as a spy had more allure than journalism, so Wiskemann decided in early 1940 to join the British legation in Switzerland. From 1941 to 1945, she worked in Bern for the Political Intelligence Department, which later became the Political Warfare Executive (PWE), one of Britain's nine secret services of the Second World War. The PWE, which specialized in what it called "black propaganda," needed an ex-journalist like Wiskemann who thrived on validating gossip and rumors about Hitler's regime. Her cover was that she was working in Berne as an assistant press attaché, but she reported only to the legation chief for Britain in Switzerland.[6]

Wiskemann was only the second woman to be granted full diplomatic rank by the Foreign Office, a status she insisted upon before taking the job. The information and rumors she gathered were not about troop movements, armaments buildups, or leaked plans of air raids. It was more societal: Who could be trusted or not, how much did the German populace knew about the Reich's goals, how many people turned out for Reich rallies, what communication channels were safe to use, where was anti-Nazi sentiment growing in Europe, and what new actions against Jews were the Nazis taking? Her sources included businessmen, bankers, artists, writers, actresses, and Berlin newspaper correspondents.

Gathering and checking on the truth of gossip was her daily routine. In Bern, for three years, she lived in a "pleasant flat," as she called it, on the top floor of an apartment building. She purposely chose it for its lack of a concierge, so visitors could come and go undetected. There were German spies everywhere in the city. She had a season ticket on the Federal Railways and at a moment's notice would rush off to Zurich, Basel, Geneva, or Lugano in Italy, hoping to hear a first-hand account of a visit to Germany. She also had a good friend at the Polish legation in Bern for news from the East. When meeting her contacts in public places, she often spoke in whispers. "I was much more careful than the Legation in general about what I said on the telephone and about what I committed to paper.[7] In Bern, she was introduced to a German Catholic journalist who frequented the German legation and wanted to help the British defeat Hitler. He came to her flat with information almost every other week during the war, providing her with "reliable and valuable information," as well as entertaining gossip about Hitler's mistress, Eva Braun. "He had his code name on the telephone, and I put special initials, not his, in my diary when he was due."[8] He is said to be Albert Kramer.[9] Initials of other friends and contacts not necessarily passing on inside information were reversed, just to be safe.

In Geneva, a hub for diplomats, journalists, and businessmen, she met Hungarians, Czechs, Belgians, Germans, and Dutch, all of whom kept on top of the latest gossip and news from home. Her universe of friends and contacts included Raymond Gautier, of an old Genevese family, who was the head of the World Health Organization. He was a conduit of news from doctors of different nationalities who came to Geneva. She also met regularly in Geneva with Carl Burckhardt, head of the International Red Cross. Wiskemann said he was "marvelously entertaining...though I felt he [was] more interested in getting things out of me than vice-versa."[10]

Wiskemann went to lengths to put her sources at ease. One was an unnamed official of the German chemical company Hoffmann-La Roche. He knew there would be trouble for him in Germany if he was seen talking with her in Switzerland, and so he only met with her after dark at his home outside Basel. Several times she missed the last tram and had to walk the six kilometers to her hotel in Basel on a snowy road near the border.

In her diary, Wiskemann disguised the real names of her sources with untraceable initials, "Y" was her Hoffmann-La Roche friend who had a Jewish wife. An anti-Nazi, he "was most informative" after he returned from Berlin and told her about anti-Nazi activities of his industrialist friends there, Wiskemann later wrote. "Back in Berne X [a German Catholic journalist working there] often confirmed what he [Y] had said."[11]

Wiskemann maintained a secret personal life, revealed in the 103 letters she sent to her lover Harry Bergholz, a German businessman living in Lausanne.[12] In one letter she wrote Bergholz in the early 1940s, she noted the difficulties of scheduling their next rendezvous because her London handlers "want me to go on trying to collect other stuff, so I must dash about for half days sometimes." Elizabeth and Harry were single at the time, and other letters show that following the war they maintained a platonic friendship after Harry married and had a daughter.

Wiskemann and a British legation colleague in Bern compared notes in mid-1941 on what they had heard about poison gas being used in experiments on Jews already dying of incurable diseases in Germany. Her source had been a Jewish banker whose German wife knew of the experiments. When Wiskemann heard some months later in 1941 from the banker that a "final solution" of mass killings with gas was in the works, she reported it to British officials. They had heard similar warnings from Jewish leaders. This was before the Nazis formally adopted the "Final Solution" in January 1942.

She had the most in common with fellow spy Allen Dulles, head of the Office of Secret Services (OSS) in Bern. It was a civilian intelligence agency that was the precursor to the Central Intelligence Agency, which Dulles subsequently headed. Wiskemann had met him in New York, in 1938, and when he moved to Bern in 1942, she was eager to build a mutually beneficial relationship comparing sources and opinions. She passed on tips about possible German spies but didn't always follow his advice. Dulles, a staunch anti-Communist, told her not to believe favorable comments she had heard about Communist leader, Josip Broz Tito. She decided "to report a bit of what I found convincing about the Tito story nevertheless," and was glad to see the British backing Tito some months later in 1943.

Dulles, the younger brother of future Secretary of State John Foster Dulles, frequented Wiskemann's apartment near his office for clandestine meetings and reciprocated by inviting her to his home for dinner or lunch on weekends. After one dinner, aware of the Swiss system of rationing, she sent him a note saying, "Dear Mr. Dulles, I'm suffering from a little guilty conscience about all those nice meals in your house...I herewith send you a few little yellow coupons (rationing stamps). Even if you don't need them, it makes me feel better."[13] Sharing information they both needed was a two-way street. Knowing of her vast network of sources in Germany and throughout Europe, Dulles "charmed her reports out of her with flowers, flirty notes, and fancy meals his cook prepared."[14] Wiskemann, in turn, leaned on Dulles as her chief link to the US government. When she had news she thought both the British and Americans should know about, she would alert Dulles after sending her cable to London.

In her mid-forties at the war's end, she left Bern for London, where she returned to journalism as a correspondent for the *Observer* and the *Economist*. She also wrote several history books and her own memoir, *The Europe I Saw*. In 1958, the University of Edinburgh named her the Montague Burton Chair of International Relations, the first woman given the honor. With her eyesight deteriorating rapidly, Wiskemann took her own life at her London home in 1971. Her obituary in the *London Times* noted that "when the University at Oxford gave her an honorary degree, she was honored as 'a Cassandra who lived to record the war she had foretold and as a historian.'"

AFTERWORD

Arnost Rosin. Several years after the war, Arnost and his fellow escapee Ceslav Mordowicz took a motorcycle trip together, retracing their escape route from Auschwitz to Slovakia. Living under the name Stefan Rohac to avoid identification as an Auschwitz escapee, Rosin had stayed in Bratislava, married a Czech woman, and worked his way up to an official position with the state television administration. He moved to West Germany in 1968 and resided in Dusseldorf, where he died in 2000, at the age of eighty-seven.

Alfred Wetzler. Wetzler joined the Slovakian partisan resistance movement in February 1945. That same year, he published under a pseudonym, Josef Lanik, a seventy-three-page pamphlet called *Auschwitz, the Grave of Four Million People*, which chronicled the origins of the Auschwitz reports. In 1963, he wrote a memoir about his escape called *What Dante Did Not See*.[1] He was a newspaper editor, who retired due to poor health. Wetzler died in Slovakia in 1988.

Miklós Horthy. After the regent of Hungary and his family were liberated from the Bavarian castle where they were living under house arrest, Horthy was once again arrested, this time by the US Army, and charged with complicity in the "Final Solution." Taken to a prison in Nuremberg, he was asked to provide evidence against Nazi officials. Thanks to the influence of former US ambassador to Hungary, John Montgomery, as well as that of Soviet ruler Joseph Stalin, who appreciated Horthy's plan to leave the Axis partnership, Horthy was released without being tried. He then moved with his family to Bavaria, before settling in Portugal, where he wrote his memoir, *A Life for Hungary*,[2] in which he repeated his claim that, before the release of the Auschwitz Protocols, he was not aware that hundreds of thousands of Hungarian Jews were being killed at the camp. He died in 1957; his wish to be buried in Hungary was granted in 1993, when his body was returned for reburial, amidst controversy, in his hometown of Kenderes.

Adolf Eichmann. At the end of the war, US troops captured Eichmann, who at the time carried forged papers saying he was Otto Eckmann. He then escaped from a work detail at a prison camp in Germany for former SS officers. Nazi sympathizers gave him a new identity that allowed him to flee to Argentina. Nazi hunters helped Israel track Eichmann down in Buenos Aires, where Israeli security agents captured him in May 1960. In Israel, a lengthy trial followed. Just after midnight on June 1, 1961, the "bloodhound" was executed by hanging. One of his Nazi cohorts testified at the Nuremberg trials of 1946 that Eichmann said he would "leap laughing into his grave because the feeling that he had five million people on his conscience would be for him a source of great satisfaction."

Edmund Veesenmayer. Surprisingly, the Reich plenipotentiary in Hungary got off lightly in the war crimes trials.

Although he was one of those most responsible for the Holocaust in Hungary, his sentence of twenty years in prison, imposed after his conviction at the Nuremberg Ministries Trial, was quickly commuted to ten and then, two years later, he was released. The US high commissioner for Germany and a special US clemency board reportedly opted for leniency to improve US-German relations after the war.[3] Veesenmayer died at the age of seventy-three in 1977.

Ferenc Szálasi. The trial of Szálasi and eight of his close associates began in December 1945. They were charged with being responsible for having ruined Hungary when they prevented Horthy from leaving the Axis alliance. It gave the prosecution the opportunity to trace the background of the Nyilas movement, its relationship with the Nazi Party, and the murders it carried out during the six months prior to the liberation of the country. All the accused were convicted and condemned to death.[4]

Domë Sztójay. The former minister president of Hungary and four members of his government were accused of sacrificing the interests of the nation by collaborating with the Third Reich. The trials, which began in March 1946, focused on the eagerness of his government to satisfy the Nazi goal of eliminating the Jewish race from Hungary.[5] All of them were found guilty. A firing squad executed Sztójay and three of his co-defendants; the other served life imprisonment.

Andor Jaross, László Baky, László Endre. In December 1945, the widely reported trial of Minister of the Interior Jaross and his two secretaries of state for Jewish affairs revealed the planning and implementation of the "Final Solution" in Hungary. It took only three weeks for the so-called "deportation trio" to be found guilty and sentenced to death. Baky and Endre were hanged on March 29. Jaross was shot by a firing squad on April 11, 1946.[6]

László Ferenczy. The head of the Hungarian army's gendarmerie fled to Germany in 1945, where he was apprehended by the US Army and extradited to Hungary to stand trial. The charge of crimes against humanity stemmed from his oversight of the gendarmerie troops in ghettoizing and deporting more than 400,000 Hungarian Jews. He was sentenced to death and hanged on March 31, 1946.

Carl Lutz. Lutz returned to Switzerland, divorced his wife, and in 1949 married Magda Csanyi who, during the war, had asked him to protect her and her daughter.[7] Lutz remained an unknown hero to most of his countrymen for years, but Israel and several other countries recognized his deeds; a street in Haifa is named after him. He died in 1975. Twenty years later, the Swiss federal government declared that Lutz had been one of the country's most outstanding citizens.[8]

Raoul Wallenberg. Eichmann and his cohorts in Hungary couldn't capture the savior of so many Jews, who evaded them by staying in different houses. But the Soviets turned on him when he sought their assistance. The day before the Russian army liberated Budapest, Wallenberg is said to have traveled outside the city seeking help from them for Budapest's Jews. A day later, on January 18, 1945, Soviets responded to Swiss inquiries that he was under Soviet protection. Then in 1957, after persistent inquiries, the Soviet Union said he had died in prison of a heart attack ten years earlier. But reports surfaced that he had been seen alive in the Soviet prison system.[9]

Rev. Angelo Rotta. He retired from diplomacy in 1957 and lived in Rome, where he died in 1965 at the age of ninety-three. The Yad Vashem Institute in Jerusalem named him one of the "Righteous Gentiles" in 1997, an honor also given to Lutz and Wallenberg.

ACKNOWLEDGMENTS

Knowledgeable, helpful sources were the lifeline to my career in journalism. And so it was in this endeavor. The writing, editing, and publication could not have taken place without the kind advice from and research by the following people and organizations. Some of them may not recall my calls for assistance, but they will always have my gratitude for their friendly and professional responses.

I owe my interest in Ceslav's escape to Union College history professor Stephen Berk and to learning of his interest from Ben Haimowitz.

My link to finding the publisher of this book came my longtime friend Judy Hottensen and George Gibson, a work colleague. Her wise advice and encouragement kept me in the hunt until George spotted the news about a new Jewish publishing imprint named Wicked Son.

Adam Bellow, Founder of Wicked Son, gave invaluable editing suggestions. I owe the smooth handling of each step of the production process to Post Hill Press Managing Editor, Heather King.

Dagmar Wertheim, Ceslav's daughter, welcomed me into her Toronto home for several visits with Ceslav in 1995 and continued to be a valued resource filling in gaps of Ceslav's life not covered elsewhere.

Esther Gilbert, widow of the late historian Martin Gilbert, graciously shared Sir Martin's files with me and made numerous introductions to valuable sources.

Lee Smith, a gifted freelance editor, asked me just the right questions to sharpen the tone and structure of my manuscript. Many thanks to my friends Will Blythe and Mike Carroll for putting me in touch with Lee.

Randolph L. Braham, the renowned Hungarian Holocaust historian, encouraged me to be "scholarly" in my research. He died in 2018 before I could take him up on his generous offer to read my manuscript.

Other writers whose works included aspects of the Holocaust and who gave me valuable advice and/or introductions were Peter Kamber, David Kertzer, Zoltan Tibori Szabo, Anne Heller, Susan Faludi, Anna Porter, Frank Baron, Robert Jan Van Pelt, Jan Hlivinka, and John Lamperti.

Agnes Kaposi, Gerta Vrbova (deceased), Avi Pazner (son of Chaim Pozner), and Holocaust survivors Dr. John Merey and Manny Buchman each shared useful recollections. And Amy Quint who saved the day in the home stretch of this book with a vital computer transmission solution.

Riva Atlas, Margaret Shannon, Sara Palmor, and Nikola Zimring researched or translated pivotal archival documents.

I am immensely grateful to the following Holocaust museums, photo archives, and libraries for the work they do and for sharing their information. Names of officials and staff who pointed me in the right direction or retrieved what I needed are:

The United States Holocaust Memorial Museum, Peter Black, Judith Cohen, and Rebeca Erbelding.

FDR Presidential Library and Museum, Kirsten Carter and Kendra Lightner.

Harvard Law School Library, Nuremberg Trials Project, Paul Deschner.

Dorot Jewish Division, New York Public Library, Reference Desk staff.

Auschwitz-Birkenau Memorial and Museum, Wojciech Plosa, Szymon Kowakski, Piotr Setklewicz, and Lukasz Lipinski.

Swiss Federal Archives, Katja Zuercher-Maeder, Guido Koller, and Melina Gnagi.

Ministry of Foreign Affairs, Czech Republic, Helena Balounova, Michaela Iagronova.

Ministry of Foreign Affairs, Germany, Gerhard Keiper.

National Archives of Hungary Laszlo Csosz and Adam Torok.

Yad Vashem, Emanuel Saunders

The Simon Wiesenthal Center, Margo Gutstein, and Susie Mamzhi.

Churchill Archives Centre, Churchill College, Cambridge University, Heidi Egginton.

Granger Historical Picture Archive, Ellen Pearlman.

Newnham College, Cambridge University, Anne Thompson.

University of Edinburgh, Paul Barnaby.

World Zionist Organization, Rochelle Rubinstein.

Moreshet Archive, Daniela Ozacky.

Getty Images NA, staff.

And, of course, the dozens of books written about or with prominent mention of Hungary's role in the Holocaust, the Auschwitz Protocols, and the Vrba/Wetzler, Mordowicz/Rosin escapes provided the basis for my research and evaluation in relation to information from other sources named above. The conclusions and points of view in the final rendering of this book are entirely my own. If they add to or clarify some debatable facts and shine more light on the importance of Ceslav's role I will have accomplished my mission.

Despite all the help and encouragement I received, no one was more important than Jane Berentson, my wife of thirty-five years whose everyday wit, cheerful outlook, and understanding of challenges kept me focused on the elusive light that finally came into view.

BIBLIOGRAPHY

Baron, Frank. *Stopping the Trains to Auschwitz, Budapest, 1944*. University of Kansas Jayhawk Ink, 2020.

Borkin, Joseph. *The Crime and Punishment of I. G. Farben*. New York: The Free Press (a division of Macmillan), 1978.

Braham, Randolph L. *The Destruction of Hungarian Jewry: A Documentary Account*, two vols. New York: Pro Arte Publishing, for the World Federation of Hungarian Jews, 1963.

———. *The Politics of Genocide*, two vols. New York: Columbia University Press, third revised edition, 2016.

Braham, ed. *The Tragedy of Hungarian Jewry*. New York: Columbia University Press, 1986.

———. *Studies on the Holocaust in Hungary*. New York: Columbia University Press, 1990.

Braham and vanden Heuvel, eds. The Auschwitz Reports. New York: Columbia University Press, 2011.

Carter, Kit C., and Robert Mueller, compilers. *The Army Air Forces in World War II: Combat Chronology, 1941-1945*. Washington: for sale by the Superintendent of Documents, US Government Printing Office, 1973.

Czech, Danuta. *Auschwitz Chronicle 1939-1945*. New York: Owl Book, Henry Holt and Co., 1997.

Erbelding, Rebecca. *Rescue Board*. New York: Anchor Books, Penguin Random House, 2019.

Fairweather, Jack. *The Volunteer*. New York: Harper Collins, 2019

Faludi, Susan. *In the Darkroom*. New York: Picador, Henry Holt and Company, 2016.

Feingold, Henry L. *Bearing Witness*. Syracuse, NY: Syracuse University Press, 1995.

Garnett, David. *The Secret History of PWE*. London: St. Ermin's Press, 2002.

Gilbert, Martin. *The Holocaust*. New York: Holt Paperbacks (a division of Henry Holt and Co.), 1985.

———. *Churchill & the Jews*. New York: Henry Holt and Co., 2007.

———. *The Righteous*. New York: Doubleday, 2002.

———. *Auschwitz and the Allies*. London: Pimlico, Random House, paperback ed., 2001.

Gutman, Israel, and Michael Beenbaum, eds. *Anatomy of the Auschwitz Death Camp*. Bloomington, IN: Indiana University Press, 1998.

Heller, Anne, C. *Hannah Arendt: A Life in Dark Times*. Boston: New Harvest, Houghton Mifflin, Harcourt, 2015.

Hirschi, Agnes, and Charlotte Schaillié, eds. *Under Swiss Protection*. Stuttgart: Ibidem Press, 2017.

Hlavinka, Jan, and Hana Kubota, eds. *Uncovering the Shoa: Resistance of Jews and Their Efforts to Inform the World on Genocide*. Bratislava: Institute of History of the Slovak Academy of Sciences, 2016.

Horthy, Miklós. *A Life for Hungary: Memoirs*. New York: Robert Speeler & Sons, 1957.

Kranzler, David. *The Man Who Stopped the Trains to Auschwitz*. Syracuse, NY: Syracuse University Press, 2000.

Lacqueur, Walter. *The Terrible Secret*. New York: Owl Books (a division of Henry Holt and Co.), 1998.

Larson, Eric. *In the Garden of the Beasts*. New York: Broadway Books, 2011.

Levai, Jeno. *Hungarian Jewry and the Papacy*. London: Sands & Co., Ltd., 1965.

———. *Black Book*. Zurich: Central European Times Publishing Co., 1948.

———. *Eichmann in Hungary*. New York: Howard Fertig, paperback ed., 2014.

Levine, Alan, J. *Captivity, Flight, and Survival in World War II*. Westport, CT: Praeger, 2000.

Levy, Alan. *The Wiesenthal File*. London: Constable and Co. Ltd., 1993.

Montgomery, John F. *Hungary: The Unwilling Satellite*. Arcole Publishing, 2017, originally published in 1947.

Morris, Heather. *The Tattooist of Auschwitz*. New York: Harper, 2018.

Munkacsi, Erno. *How It Happened*. Edited by Nina Munk. Montreal: McGill-Queen's University Press, 2018.

Patai, Raphael, *The Jews of Hungary*, Detroit: Wayne State University Press, 1996.

Porter, Anna. *Kasztner's Train*. New York: Walker Publishing, 2007.

Rosenberg, Joel, C. *The Auschwitz Escape*. Carol Stream, IL: Tyndale House Publishers, 2014.

Seba, Anne. *Battling for News*. London: Sceptre (a division of Hodder & Stoughton), 1995.

Stangeth, Bettina. *Eichmann Before Jerusalem: The Unexamined Life of a Mass Murderer*. New York: Alfred A. Knopf, 2014.

Suhl, Yuri, ed. and trans. *They Fought Back*. New York: Crown Publishers, 1967.

Świebocki, Henryk, ed. *London Has Been Informed*. Oswiecim, Poland: Auschwitz-Birkenau State Museum, 2002.

———. *Auschwitz, 1940–1945: Central Issues in the History of the Camp, Vol. IV: The Resistance Movement*. Oświęcim: Auschwitz-Birkenau State Museum, 2000.

Tschuy, Theo. *Dangerous Diplomacy: The Story of Carl Lutz*. Grand Rapids, MI: William B. Eerdmans, 2000.

Ungvary, Krisztian. *The Siege of Budapest*. New Haven: Yale University Press, 2005.

Vagi, Zoltan, László Csosz, and Gabor Kadar. *The Holocaust in Hungary*. Plymouth, UK: AltaMira Press (a division of Rowman and Littlefield Publishers), 2013.

Vrba, Rudolf, and Alan Bestic. *I Cannot Forgive*. Vancouver: Regent College Publishing, expanded 1997 edition; originally published 1963.

———. *I Escaped from Auschwitz*. Fort Lee, NJ: Barricade Books, 2002.

———. *I Escaped from Auschwitz*. New York: Racehorse Publishing, 2020.

Vrbova, Gerta. *Betrayed Generation*. Great Britain: Zuza Books, 2006.

Waller, Douglas. *Disciples: The World War II Missions of the CIA Directors Who Fought for Wild Bill Donovan*. New York: Simon & Schuster, 2015.

Wetzler, Alfred. *Escape from Hell*. New York: Berghahn Books, first paperback, 2020; originally published as *What Dante Did Not See* in 1963.

———. Oswiecim. HROBKA STYROCH MILLIONOV LUDI. (*Auschwitz: The Tomb of Four Million People.*) A 72-page pamphlet in Slovakian language, edited by Jozko Lanik, Alfred Wetzler's penname. Written by AW (Alfred Wetzler), Rudolf Vrba, Arnost Rosin, and Ceslav Mordowicz. Bratislava. SNR Commission for Information. 1945.

Wiskemann, Elizabeth, *The Europe I Saw.* New York: St. Martin's Press, 1968.

Wiesel, Elie. *Night.* New York: Hill & Wang (a division of Farrar, Straus and Giroux), 1986.

Wohlforth, William. *Deadly Imbalances: Tripolarity and Hitler's Strategy of World Conquest.* New York: Columbia University Press, 1998.

Wyman, David S. *The Abandonment of the Jews.* New York: The New Press, 2007 edition.

ENDNOTES

Introduction

1 Ceslav, without the z and w (Czeslaw, his Polish name) is the Slovakian vernacular name he assumed for life when he went to Bratislava.

2 Reitlinger, *The Final Solution*, first paragraph of Chapter 16, "Hungary."

3 Braham, *The Destruction of Hungarian Jewry*, vol. 1, LXXVII. A "lightning strike" was planned for one day in early to mid-July. Eberhard von Thadden, a German Foreign Ministry specialist for the "Final Solution," had outlined the plan for Budapest in a secret report to Berlin headquarters on May 26, 1944: "From the middle of July..., they (The SS) think they can start in Budapest itself. For this purpose, a one-day major action is planned to be carried out using strong Hungarian gendarmerie from the provinces, all special units and police, as well as using all the Budapest postmen and chimney sweeps as pilots. The entire bus and tram traffic will be stopped on this day, in order to use all means of transport for the deportation of the Jews." As concern about Horthy's loyalty to Germany grew, the Nazis advanced the "lightning strike" target date to July 7.

4 Braham, *The Politics of Genocide*, 967. Noting that the pope's plea to Hungary's leader Miklós Horthy on June 25, 1944, followed by the warning of President Roosevelt on June 26 and that of King Gustav of Sweden on June 30, Braham wrote that "there is no doubt that these communications played an important, if not determining, role in Horthy's decision to prohibit further deportations from Hungary."

5 Fred R. Bleakley, "An Unsung Hero of Auschwitz," *Wall Street Journal*, June 12, 1995.

6 Ceslav Mordowicz. The author met Ceslav Mordowicz on June 11, 1995, in Schenectady, New York, at the commencement exercise of Union College, where he was awarded an honorary degree. They subsequently had several lengthy interviews in Toronto at the home of Ceslav's daughter Dagmar Wertheim on September 9 and 10, 1995, and October 13, 1997.

Chapter Three

1 From a 72-page booklet, *Auschwitz: Tomb of Four Million People*, the four escapees (Vrba, Wetzler, Mordowicz, and Rosin) wrote in the summer of 1944 to personalize and reinforce the Auschwitz Protocols sent to Switzerland in May and June. See Bibliography.

2 Braham, *Destruction of Hungarian Jewry*, vol. 1, LV, Doc. 66.

3 Heller, *Hannah Arendt*, 85–87.

ENDNOTES

Chapter Four

1 Henryk Świebocki, ed., *Auschwitz, 1940–1945: Central Issues in the History of the Camp*, vol. IV: *The Resistance Movement* (Oświęcim: Auschwitz-Birkenau State Museum, 2000), 232–233.

Chapter Five

1 Levai, *Eichmann in Hungary*, 101.
2 Peter Black, chief historian, US Holocaust Memorial Museum from 1997 to 2016, correspondence in reply to questions from the author, May 3, 2021.
3 Faludi, *In the Darkroom*, 110–111.
4 Montgomery, *Hungary: The Unwilling Satellite*, 40.
5 Horthy, *Memoirs*, n.d., 162.
6 Ibid.
7 Ibid.
8 Wohlforth, *Deadly Imbalances*, 78–79.
9 Patai, *The Jews of Hungary*, 546. Miklós Horthy: "As regards the Jewish problem, I have been an anti-Semite throughout my life. I have never had contact with Jews. I have considered it intolerable that here in Hungary everything, every factory, bank, large fortune, business, theatre, press, commerce, etc. should be in Jewish hands, and that the Jew should be the image reflected of Hungary, especially abroad. Since, however, one of the most important tasks of the government is to raise the standard of living, i.e., we have to acquire wealth, it is impossible, in a year or two, to replace the Jews, who have everything in their hands, and to replace them with incompetent, unworthy, mostly big-mouthed elements, for we should become bankrupt. This requires a generation at least."
10 Levai, 54.
11 Ibid, 64.
12 Horthy, 213.
13 Ibid.

Chapter Six

1 Munkacsi, *How It Happened*, 19.
2 Levy, *The Wiesenthal File*, 118.
3 Levai, *Eichmann in Hungary*, 69.
4 Vagi, Csosz, and Kadar, *The Holocaust in Hungary*, 256.
5 Munkacsi, 57.
6 Ibid.
7 Csosz, Laszlo and Szeghy-Gayer, Veronika. "Petitioners of Jewish Property in Kocice..." Institute of Contemporary History, Czech Academy of Sciences. Praha, Czech Republic. *The City History*, vol. 10, 84, 2021.
8 Braham, *Politics of Genocide*, 625.
9 Ibid, 627.
10 Levai, 74.
11 Ibid, 87–88.
12 Czech, *Auschwitz Chronicle*, 618.
13 Gilbert, *The Holocaust*, 671.
14 Levai, 91.
15 Ibid, 92.
16 Ibid, 104.
17 Gilbert, 679.
18 Erbelding, *Rescue Board*, 133.
19 Munkacsi, *How It Happened*, 139.
20 Ibid, 140.
21 Ibid.
22 Gilbert, 681.
23 Ibid, 675. Eyewitness account from Alter Feinsilber, one of the few survivors of the Auschwitz Jewish *Sonderkommando*.

Chapter Seven

1 Auschwitz-Birkenau State Museum, APMA-B, IZ-8/Gestapo Lodz/4, Gestapo Litzmannstadt, Telegramy o ucieczkach, vol. 5, p. 117–118; Evelin Verhás, Angéla Kóczé, and Anna Lujza Szász (eds.), *Roma Resistance during the Holocaust and in Its Aftermath*, Collection of Working Papers, Tom Lantos Institute, Budapest, 2018.

Chapter Eight

1 Braham, *Politics of Genocide*, vol. 2, 961.
2 Gilbert, *Auschwitz and the Allies*, 203–204.

3 Braham, vol. 2, *Destruction of Hungarian Jewry*, 912–913; testimony of Dr. Rezsö (Rudolf) Kastner, September 13, 1945.

4 Gilbert, 231–232, footnote 3, Oskar Krasnansky, conversation with Gilbert, Tel Aviv, December 22, 1980; Kulka, "Five Escapes from Auschwitz," from *They Fought Back*.

5 The following account of the Vrba/Wetzler escape highlights some of the more dramatic moments from a 2020 expanded version, "I Escaped From Auschwitz," of Vrba's earlier memoir.

6 Vrba, *I Escaped from Auschwitz* (New York: Simon & Schuster, 2002), Essay by Professor John S. Conway of the University of British Columbia, 289–324.

7 Braham, *The Politics of Genocide*, 966.

8 Ernest (Arnost) Rosin, telephone interview with author and Professor Stephen Berk of Union College, translated by Carl Rosner, April 11, 1996.

9 Mordowicz, conversation in Toronto with the author, September 9, 1995.

10 Mrs. Gabor Munk, July 29, 1944, letter provided to the author by her grandson, John H. Merey, MD, an ophthalmologist in West Palm Beach, Florida, on March 2, 2018. Dr. Merey, Mrs. Munk, and twelve others in their extended family escaped Hungary when Dr. Merey's uncle paid for them to be passengers on the so-called "Kasztner's Train" arranged by the Orthodox Rabbi Dr. Rudolf Kasztner with Eichmann.

11 Vagi, Csosz, and Kadar, *Holocaust in Hungary*, 112–115.

Chapter Nine

1 Kranzler, *The Man Who Stopped*, 85.

2 Ibid, 88.

3 Ibid, 89; Kranzler said in footnotes that he interviewed Mantello several times for the book.

4 Ibid, 91.

5 Ibid, 92.

6 Avi Pazner (son of Chaim Pozner), telephone interview, Tel Aviv, October 5, 2017.

7 Tschuy, *Dangerous Diplomacy*, 141.

8 Kranzler, 115.

9 Sir Martin Gilbert, "Bombing Auschwitz: Fact & Myth," *Finest Hour: The Journal of Winston Churchill*, May 11, 2005; copy in Gilbert archives at Hillsdale College, Hillsdale, Michigan. Gilbert, *Churchill and the Jews*, 212.

10 Feingold, *Bearing Witness*, 289, footnote 40. Feingold's footnote said the seventy names attachment could be found at the FDR Library in two telegrams from McClelland to WRB head John Pehle on June 24 and July 24. The archivists at the FDR Library could not find the footnote reference. Similarly, US Holocaust Memorial Museum does not have such an attachment in its WRB files. It is possible the information was redacted because it could be considered libelous to some of the persons named.

11 As noted in the previous endnote, there is no attachment of the seventy names and addresses in the WRB files.

Chapter Ten

1 Sir Martin Gilbert, "Bombing Auschwitz: Fact & Myth," *Finest Hour: The Journal of Winston Churchill*, May 11, 2005; copy in Gilbert archives at Hillsdale College, Hillsdale, Michigan. Gilbert, *Churchill and the Jews*, 212.

2 Carter and Mueller, compilers, *US Army Air Forces in World War II: Combat Chronology, 1941–1945*, 387.

3 Kranzler, *The Man Who Stopped*, 117.

4 Ibid, 116.

5 Braham, *Politics of Genocide*, vol. 2, 1020.

6 Ibid.

7 David Kertzer, Brown University professor of Italian studies, email message to author, May 24, 2018.

8 Vagi, Csosz, and Kadar, *The Holocaust in Hungary*, 135.

9 Levai, *Black Book*, 248.

10 Munkasci, *How It Happened*, 210.

11 Levai, Ibid.

12 Veesenmayer telegram, Office of Chief Counsel for War Crimes, Nuremberg

Trials Project, Cambridge, Massachusetts, Harvard Law School, Translation of Document No. NG - 5684.
13 Ibid, Document No. NG - 5523.
14 Levai, 252.

Chapter Eleven
1 Levai, *Eichmann in Hungary*, 127–8.
2 Ibid.
3 Krantzler, *The Man Who Stopped*, 158.
4 Braham, *The Destruction of Hungarian Jewry*, vol. 1, CX, Doc. 326.
5 Ibid, LXXXV, Doc. 199.
6 Kranzler, 194.
7 Levai, 144.
8 Miklós Horthy, Wikipedia.
9 Gilbert, *The Righteous*, 337.
10 Braham, *The Destruction*, XCI, Doc. 226.
11 Levai, 146.
12 Ibid.
13 Braham, *The Politics of Genocide*, vol. 2, 1115–1117.
14 Feingold, *Bearing Witness*, 166.
15 Braham, 1127.
16 Braham, *Destruction of Hungarian Jewry*, vol. 2, 899.
17 Tschuy, *Dangerous Diplomacy: The Story of Carl Lutz*, foreword by Nazi hunter Simon Wiesenthal.
18 Ibid.
19 Kranzler, *The Man Who Stopped*, 188.
20 Wyman, *Abandonment*, 242.
21 Levai, 180.
22 Braham, *The Politics of Genocide*, vol. 2, 1169, 1170.
23 Ibid, 1507.

Chapter Twelve
1 Mordowicz. US Holocaust Memorial Museum. Oral Interview, Oct. 30, 1996, p. 54–55, RG-50.030*0354
2 The report was not included in the War Refugee Board's November 1944 public disclosure of the Auschwitz Protocols, but was published as a 72-page pamphlet in 1945 in Slovakia as Oswiecim. HROBKA STYROCH MILLIONOV LUDI. SPRACOVAL (*Auschwitz: The Tomb of Four Million*

People) with the authors' names listed on the first page.
3 Oswiecim, HROBKA STYROCH MILLIONOV LUDI. SPRACOVAL: Jozko Lanik, SNR pre Informacie. p. 62, 63, 67.
4 Mordowicz, Ibid.
5 Tibor Neumann, interview with Fred Bleakley at Neumann's Encino, California, home on September 18, 1995. Neumann and Ceslav were in the same cattle car headed toward Auschwitz that day in October 1944. They knew each other, having met that summer when Tibor's family lived next door to Ceslav and Alfred's apartment in Bratislava. Ceslav would come over in the evenings to socialize and tell of Auschwitz. Neumann was selected for labor and survived the war, moving to Los Angeles in 1948.
6 Lady Esther Gilbert (Sir Martin Gilbert's widow), email to the author, July 26, 2017.

Epilogue
1 Vrbova, *Betrayed Generation* (Great Britain: Zuza Books, 2006), 75.
2 Ibid.
3 Ibid.
4 Ibid, 74.
5 Gerta Vrbova, interview with author at her home in North London in October 2019.
6 Ibid.
7 Dagmar Wertheim, telephone interviews with author, November 17, 2017, November 4, 2019, and January 8, 2020. Responses on May 12, July 24, and July 30, 2020, by email to questions from the author.
8 Ceslav Mordowicz, an August 9, 1995, letter addressed to historian John S. Conway, following a July 25, 1995, letter Conway had written to the editor of the *Wall Street Journal*. In Conway's letter to the *WSJ*, he refuted the relevance of the Mordowicz/Rosin report cited by Professor Stephen Berk of Union College in a June 12, 1995,

WSJ article by the author, "An Unsung Hero of Auschwitz is honored by a New York College." Berk replied in his own letter to the *WSJ* letter, chastising Conway for "ignoring the role of other Auschwitz escapees." Two years later, in an essay about the Hungarian Holocaust published by the Simon Wiesenthal Center of Los Angeles, Conway did acknowledge the relevance of Mordowicz/Rosin report. "There can be no doubt that the breaking of the conspiracy of silence, which the Germans and their collaborators had tried to maintain, was due to the widespread publication of the reports supplied by the four escapees."

9 Eduard Niznansky, "History of the Escape of Arnost Rosin and Czeslav Mordowicz from the Auschwitz-Birkenau Concentration Camp to Slovakia in 1944," 125, taken from *Uncovering the Shoa: Resistance of Jews and Their Efforts to Inform the World on Genocide*, Ján Hlavinka and Hans Kubotova (eds.), Bratislava: Institute of History of the Slovak Academy of Sciences; Prague: International Christian Embassy Jerusalem, 2016.

10 Erich Kulka, "Attempts by Jewish Escapees to Stop Mass Exterminations," Jewish Social Studies, vol. 47, no. 3/4 (Summer–Autumn, 1985) Indiana University Press, 304.

11 Wertheim, Ibid.

12 Ibid.

13 Ibid.

14 Ibid.

15 Ibid.

16 Vrba, *I Escaped from Auschwitz*, 2002 edition, appendix V, 407. Of course, Vrba could have said in his original 1963 memoir that another Auschwitz escapee also spoke to the nuncio, without identifying him by name.

17 Ibid, 401.

18 Gilbert, Esther. Email to Fred Bleakley, July 26, 2017. After referencing the Czech family camp, she wrote, "The first one had been destroyed in March (1944), I, believe, and they worried the second one would be destroyed in the coming months. Vrba writes, at length, about the resistance efforts to save the first one. Yes, Rudi insisted that while in the camp they picked up conversation about Hungarian 'sausages', but he did not mention that in his memoir. It was Rosin and Mordowicz who escaped a few weeks later, in May, who had witnessed the arrival of the Hungarians."

19 Ján Hlavinka, telephone interview with author, November 8, 2019.

20 Vrba-Wetzler Memorial, http://edu. vrbawetzler.eu/lang_cs/homepage/.

CODA

1 The Auschwitz Protocols are online at www.fdrlibrary.marist.edu/archives/ collections/franklin. War Refugee Board, Series 1 General Correspondence, Box 7, German Extermination Camps (1.) German Extermination Camps—Auschwitz and Birkenau, November 26, 1944, Franklin D. Roosevelt Library, Hyde Park, New York.

2 Gilbert, *Auschwitz and the Allies*, 231, 232, 233; the Council combined the reports in communications to Switzerland in June that made their way to McClelland that month.

3 McClelland, General Correspondence of R. McClelland, Letter to War Refugee Board Director John Pehle, October 12, 1944, Franklin D. Roosevelt Library, Hyde Park, New York.

4 Swiebocki, *London Has Been Informed*, 41, 42.

5 The Auschwitz Protocols are online at www.fdrlibrary.marist.edu/archives/ collections/frankli. Records of the War Refugee Board, Series 1 General Correspondence, Box 7 German Extermination Camps (1), Franklin D. Roosevelt Library, Hyde Park, New York.

6 *Auschwitz 1940–1945: Central Issues in the History of the Camp*, vol. 3. (Oswiecim: Auschwitz-Birkenau State Museum, 2000), 205–232.

7 Ibid.
8 Ibid.
9 Braham, *The Politics of Genocide*, 1507–1508.

Profiles
MANTELLO
1 Kranzler, *The Man Who Stopped*, 10, 11.
2 Ibid, 14.
3 Ibid, 7–8.
4 Ibid, 27.
5 Ibid, 32.
6 Ibid, 232–3.
7 Ibid, 249.

WISKEMANN
1 Sebba, *Battling for News*, 78.
2 Wiskemann, *The Europe I Saw*, 242–245.
3 Elizabeth Wiskemann Biography, Newnham College Library, Cambridge University.
4 Wiskemann, *The Europe I Saw*, 57.
5 Sebba, 110.
6 Garnett, *The Secret History of PWE*, 142.

7 Wiskemann, *The Europe I Saw*, 142, 150, 158.
8 Ibid, 159.
9 Garnett.
10 Wiskemann, 140.
11 Ibid, 161.
12 Wiskemann Letters, Newnham College Library, Cambridge University.
13 Wiskemann Personal File, RG226, N. OSS files, Entry 210, Box 276, Folder 4, National Archives, Washington, DC.
14 Waller, *Disciples*, 136.

Afterword
1 Wetzler, *Escape from Hell*.
2 Horthy, *A Life for Hungary*.
3 Braham, *The Politics of Genocide*, vol. 2., 1581, footnote 128.
4 Ibid, 1538–9.
5 Ibid, 1539.
6 Ibid, 1538.
7 Wikipedia.
8 Tschuy, *Dangerous Diplomacy*, introduction by Simon Wiesenthal.
9 Wyman, *Abandonment of the Jews*, 243.